My Book of
Dinosaurs
AND
Prehistoric
Life

Author: Dr. Dean Lomax

Project Editors Olivia Stanford, Radhika Haswani
US Editor Margaret Parrish
US Executive Editor Lori Hand
Assistant Editor Niharika Prabhakar
Senior Art Editor Nidhi Mehra
Project Art Editors Lucy Sims, Rashika Kachroo
Jacket Coordinator Issy Walsh
Jacket Designers Lucy Sims, Dheeraj Arora
DTP Designers Dheeraj Singh, Vijay Kandwal
Picture Researchers Rituraj Singh, Sakshi Saluja
Assistant Production Editor Abi Maxwell
Senior Production Controller Inderjit Bhullar
Managing Editors Jonathan Melmoth, Monica Saigal
Managing Art Editors Diane Peyton Jones, Romi Chakraborty
Delhi Creative Heads Glenda Fernandes, Malavika Talukder
Publishing Manager Francesca Young
Creative Director Helen Senior
Publishing Director Sarah Larter

First American Edition, 2021
Published in the United States by DK Publishing
1450 Broadway, Suite 801, New York, NY 10018

Copyright © 2021 Dorling Kindersley Limited
DK, a Division of Penguin Random House LLC
21 22 23 24 25 10 9 8 7 6 5 4 3 2 1
001–321060–Jan/2021

A catalog record for this book is available from the Library of Congress.
ISBN 978-0-7440-2653-5

DK books are available at special discounts when purchased in bulk for sales promotions, premiums, fund-raising, or educational use. For details, contact: DK Publishing Special Markets, 1450 Broadway, Suite 801, New York, NY 10018
SpecialSales@dk.com

Printed and bound in China

For the curious
www.dk.com

Contents

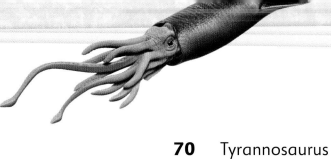

The moon formed during a collision between Earth and another small planet, called Theia. The debris from this impact became the moon.

For hundreds of millions of years, early Earth was bombarded by asteroids and meteors. They blasted countless craters in the ground.

Early Earth was extremely hot and covered with volcanoes and lava. It was also blanketed in gas clouds that helped to create the atmosphere.

Where did life come from?

Figuring out exactly where life came from is one of science's most challenging problems. Early Earth was very hot, and there was little oxygen. Scientists generally agree that life began in the water and that all life evolved from tiny microbes.

Origin of life

How life began remains one of the most difficult questions to answer. A flash of lightning may have sparked life into existence, or a chemical reaction underwater may have caused it. Another theory is that tiny microbes were brought to Earth on meteors.

Water played a crucial role in creating the perfect conditions to support life. As Earth cooled, water condensed and formed huge oceans.

Life may have begun around deep-sea hydrothermal vents. These pump out scalding-hot water that is rich in minerals from deep within the Earth.

Stromatolites are rocks formed by blue-green algae, which may have been among the Earth's first life-forms. The oldest stromatolite fossils are 3.5 billion years old.

Types of life

From single-celled bacteria to gigantic mammals, organisms come in all shapes and sizes. The main types of life can be grouped into animals, plants, fungi, and microorganisms, all of which are separated further into smaller families. All of these groups have existed for hundreds of millions of years.

Einiosaurus

Microorganisms and fungi

Microorganisms are so small that you can only see them with a microscope. Some, such as the algae called diatoms, have just one cell. Fungi include microorganisms such as yeasts and molds, along with larger organisms, such as mushrooms and toadstools.

Diatom

Toadstool

99.9% of all species that have ever lived are now extinct.

Walchia tree

Animals

The first animals appeared more than 500 million years ago. Fossil discoveries tell us that some prehistoric animals, such as the frilled dinosaur Einiosaurus or the rhinoceros-like Uintatherium, were very different to anything alive today.

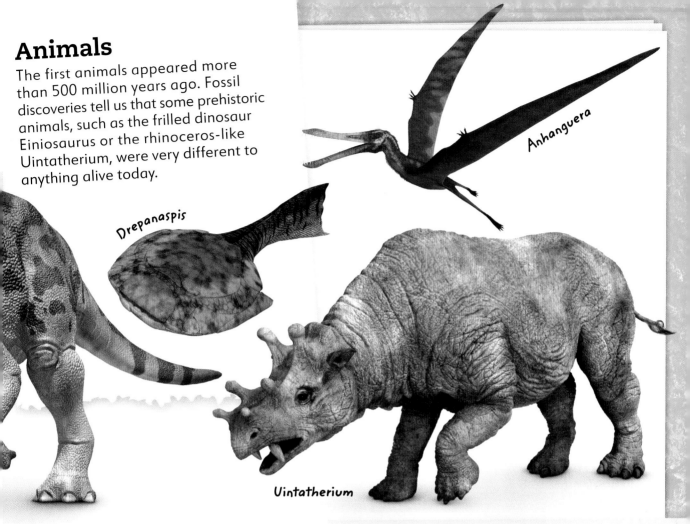

Anhanguera

Drepanaspis

Uintatherium

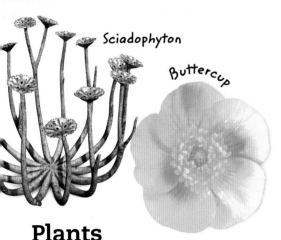

Sciadophyton

Buttercup

Plants

The first plants lived in water, but about 500 million years ago they began to grow on land as well. Prehistoric plants, such as Sciadophyton, played an important role in helping to pump oxygen into the atmosphere.

Evolution

Two 19th-century naturalists, Charles Darwin and Alfred Russel Wallace, separately came up with the theory of evolution. This theory explains how animals and plants change and develop into different forms over many generations.

The first amphibians to walk on land evolved from fish.

Timeline

Not all prehistoric animals lived at the same time. Earth's ancient history is divided into chunks called eras, which are further separated into periods. These create a timeline that helps us to understand which animals lived together and when they were alive.

Bacteria

3,500–542 MYA

First life

The earliest living organisms were microscopic bacteria. Their ancient fossils are at least 3.5 billion years old.

Brachiosaurus

Eoraptor

201–146 MYA

Jurassic

The first truly enormous dinosaurs appeared during this period. Tiny mammals lived in their shadows, scurrying along the ground and climbing up trees.

252–201 MYA

Triassic

The Permian extinction led to the evolution of many new animals, including ichthyosaurs in the sea, pterosaurs in the sky, and dinosaurs on the land.

299–252 MYA

Permian

Reptiles continued to flourish and they became the dominant land animals in the Permian, but this period ended with the largest mass extinction of all time.

Basilosaurus

Alxasaurus

146–66 MYA

Cretaceous

Dinosaurs dominated the Cretaceous, but everything changed with the impact of an enormous asteroid. The first flowers also appeared.

66–23 MYA

Paleogene

Life slowly recovered after the devastating effects of the asteroid, and mammals flourished. In the seas, the mighty marine reptiles were replaced by early whales.

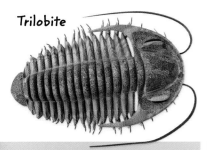
Trilobite

542–485 MYA

Cambrian

Many major groups of animals first appeared during what is known as the "Cambrian Explosion," including animals with hard outer skeletons.

Astraspis

485–444 MYA

Ordovician

In the Ordovician Period, seas were teeming with new life-forms, including many types of primitive jawless fish, such as Astraspis.

Cooksonia

444–419 MYA

Silurian

Coral reefs stretched throughout the warm Silurian seas, and plants, including Cooksonia, spread across the land.

Scutosaurus

Fern

359–299 MYA

Carboniferous

In the Carboniferous, vast tropical swamps covered the land and giant creepy-crawlies ate the lush plants. Car-sized amphibians appeared and the first reptiles evolved.

Tiktaalik

419–359 MYA

Devonian

During the Devonian Period, amphibians with four limbs evolved from fish and took their first steps out of the water and onto the land.

Deinotherium

Tiger

23–3 MYA

Neogene

Many modern types of animal appeared in the Neogene, such as Deinotherium—an early elephant. The first ancestors of humans also evolved.

3 MYA–today

Quaternary

We live in the Quaternary. Some famous mammals, such as mammoths, have become extinct, but many new species that we know today have evolved.

How old is the Earth?

Geologists estimate the Earth to be a staggering 4.54 billion years old. The rock shown here is from Jack Hills in Australia and contains minerals that are 4.4 billion years old!

Oldest material on Earth

How has Earth changed?

The Earth has changed dramatically over the course of its exceptionally long 4.54-billion-year history. Mountains have risen and crumbled, seas have come and gone, and huge supercontinents have collided and drifted apart.

Supercontinents are enormous landmasses.

In the Archaean, most of the Earth was covered in ocean.

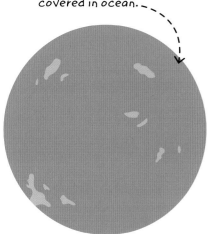

Archaean

The continents began to form during the Archaean Eon, which lasted from 4 to 2.5 billion years ago. Life existed entirely on a microscopic scale, and oceans were ruled by colonies of slimy algae.

Cambrian

The Cambrian Period began the Paleozoic Era and an explosion of life on Earth. The breakup of a previous supercontinent left behind lots of smaller continents and one supercontinent called Gondwana.

Carboniferous

During the Carboniferous Period, the continents continued to move. They formed the supercontinent Pangaea, which stretched almost from pole to pole. It was surrounded by a super-ocean named Panthalassa.

Tectonic plates

The top layers of rock that make up the Earth are split into chunks called tectonic plates. These plates move constantly over the liquid rock below them, and they may pull apart, collide, or slide past each other. As they move, they also change the shape and location of the continents that sit on top of them.

A valley caused by two tectonic plates pulling apart in Thingvellir National Park, Iceland

Parts of Africa were underwater in the Paleogene Period.

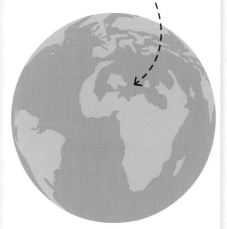

Jurassic

Mighty Pangaea started splitting up in the Jurassic Period, and more familiar-looking continents such as North America began to appear. Jurassic Earth was hot, with probably no or few ice caps and much higher sea levels.

Paleogene

During this period, the continents continued to shift and their positions became more like they are today. The Himalayan mountain range formed due to the collision of the Indian and Eurasian tectonic plates.

Today

The world today has seven major continents. These are, from largest to smallest, Asia, Africa, North America, South America, Antarctica, Europe, and Oceania. Our continents are still on the move.

Fossils

Fossils are the remains or traces of ancient life. They provide direct evidence that even long ago, Earth was populated with an enormous variety of animals and plants. Some fossils show whole skeletons of prehistoric animals.

Usually, only parts of a skeleton are preserved as fossils, although complete skeletons have been found, such as this pterosaur.

Some rare fossils show skin, fur, or feathers.

Even the most delicate parts of a skeleton can be fossilized, such as these long, slender wing bones.

During fossilization, the hard parts of the animal were replaced by minerals, turning its bones and teeth into rock.

Types of fossil

There are many different types of fossil, although paleontologists divide them into two main types: body fossils, such as bones, shells, and leaves; and trace fossils, such as tracks, nests, and dung.

This Albertosaurus skull is an example of a body fossil. It shows us what the animal looked like.

Petrified wood is another type of body fossil. You can see the texture of the bark in the remains of this branch.

Tracks are among the most common trace fossils and record a moment in time when an animal was moving.

13

Fossil formation

Only a tiny percentage of animals and plants that ever lived became fossils. Whether or not an organism becomes fossilized depends on how and where that plant or animal died. Usually only the hard parts of a life-form, such as its bones or bark, are preserved.

More than 1,500 dinosaurs have been named from fossils.

Death

Depending on how an organism died—whether of old age, by an accident, or by being eaten by a predator— either the entire animal or parts of it may become fossilized. After death, its soft parts rot away.

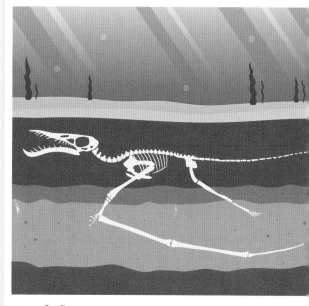

Burial

The burial process is the most important part of fossilization. The organism must have died in, or close to, water where it can become buried by mud, sand, or other sediment.

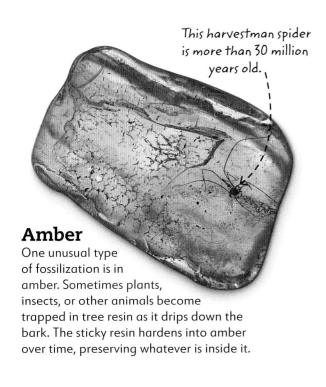

This harvestman spider is more than 30 million years old.

Amber

One unusual type of fossilization is in amber. Sometimes plants, insects, or other animals become trapped in tree resin as it drips down the bark. The sticky resin hardens into amber over time, preserving whatever is inside it.

Fossil finders

One of the earliest paleontologists was Mary Anning (1799–1847), who lived in Lyme Regis, UK. From a young age, Mary collected fossils, including an ichthyosaur she unearthed when she was just 12 years old!

Mary Anning with her dog, Tray

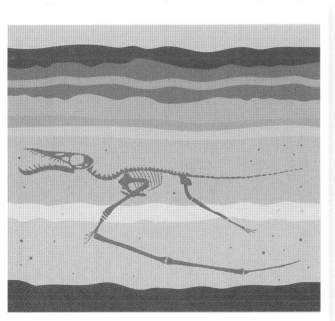

Mineralization

As the skeleton is buried deeper, its bones and teeth are slowly replaced by minerals from the surrounding sediment. This process changes the animal into a fossil.

Discovery

After millions of years, the fossil might be discovered by a fossil hunter. It can take a long time for a fossil to be excavated, as the surrounding rock has to be carefully removed.

Plants through time

Plants evolved from tiny bacteria that appeared more than 2 billion years ago. The ability of plants to transform sunlight into energy by photosynthesis helped them to spread across the land, which they began doing around 500 million years ago.

Sago palm

Cycads

Cycads first appeared in the early part of the Permian Period. During the Mesozoic Era, cycads spread to every continent, and made up about 20 percent of all plants living on land.

Ferns

The earliest ferns appeared in the Devonian Period, but they became widespread in the Carboniferous. During this period, they were one of the most dominant groups of plants, as they thrived in the vast swamps.

Fern

Mosses

The earliest plants to move from water to land would have been mosslike in appearance. Mosses, together with liverworts and hornworts, are the first land plants found as fossils.

Moss

Flowering plants

Flowering plants are the most widespread plant group today, representing about 90 percent of all living land plants. The first flowering plants evolved in the early Cretaceous Period, about 130 million years ago.

Buttercup

Spores on leaf

Cone

Flower

Seeds

Plant reproduction

Plants reproduce in a variety of ways. Some spread by dustlike spores and others produce seeds. Ancient plants made spores on their leaves or in cones and created seeds in cones or flowers.

Conifers

Conifers have been found on the Earth since the late Carboniferous Period and were the dominant land plants during the Mesozoic Era. They include the tallest living organisms ever to appear on land.

Conifer tree

Grass

Grass is found everywhere, but can you imagine a world without it? Much of the prehistoric landscape didn't have it, as it only evolved in the Cretaceous Period. Fragments of grass have been found with later dinosaur remains—even inside their droppings!

Clubmoss

Lycophytes

The lycophytes are one of the oldest living groups of vascular plants. Unlike mosses, vascular plants have special tubes inside them that are used to transport food and water around the leaves and stem.

Prairie grassland, USA

Araucaria

(a-row-KAIR-ee-a)

Araucaria is a type of conifer that is considered a "living fossil." It still grows today, but some species of this tree have been found from the Jurassic Period. One of its common names is the monkey puzzle tree.

Fact file

» **Height:** 260 ft (80 m)
» **Reproduction:** Cones with seeds
» **Period:** Jurassic
» **Location:** Asia, Europe, Oceania, and South Americ

Female

Araucaria trees reproduce with female and male cones. Seeds are made in the female cones.

Male

Pollen is made in the male cones. They are much narrower than the female cones.

Fully grown Araucaria trees have thick, tough, scalelike leaves with sharp ends.

Jet set

Jet is a type of fossilized wood made from ancient Araucaria trees. It is often carved and used in jewelry. Some of the world's finest jet comes from the Jurassic rocks of Whitby, UK.

Piece of jet

The trunk is straight, slender, and tall. Many fossilized Araucaria tree trunks have been found.

The large branches curve up at the ends. Sauropod dinosaurs would have browsed on Araucaria trees.

Williamsonia

(wil-yem-SOH-nee-a)

Williamsonia was part of a group of extinct palmlike plants, called Bennettitales, that looked like modern cycads. Although most of their fossils come from the Mesozoic Era, older and younger fossils show Bennettitales survived two mass extinctions.

» **Height:** 10 ft (3 m)
» **Reproduction:** Flowerlike cones
» **Period:** Jurassic
» **Location:** Worldwide

Clusters of long, slender fernlike fronds extended from the top of Williamsonia's trunk.

Williamsonia grew to the height of an ostrich.

The thick woody trunk had diamond-shaped scars on it where old leaves had been attached.

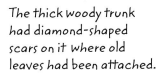

This fossilized Williamsonia cone may have been pollinated by insects.

Cycad

Cycads

Bennettitales looked similar to a group of plants called cycads. Fossils of both have been discovered but only cycads survive today. Although they resembled each other, one main difference was that the cones of Bennettitales looked like flowers.

Lycophytes
(LAI-koh-fites)

Appearing more than 400 million years ago, lycophytes were some of the first plants to develop. By the Carboniferous Period, they had changed from tiny shrublike bushes to enormous trees. They still exist, but today they are much smaller.

A single large cone containing spores grew out of the tip of the trunk.

Pleuromeia
(ploo-roh-MAY-a)

As dinosaurs began to appear, forests of Pleuromeia spread across the globe. The first Pleuromeia fossil was found accidentally in a sandstone block that was part of the Cathedral of Magdeburg in Germany.

Pleuromeia had a single trunk with no branches.

The scales on Asteroxylon were not true leaves, but they photosynthesized like the leaves of other plants.

Asteroxylon
(AS-ter-ox-y-lon)

This early land plant was one of the first lycophytes to evolve, appearing about 410 million years ago. A tough outer layer stopped Asteroxylon from drying out in the baking heat.

Sigillaria
(si-ji-LAIR-ee-a)

Sigillaria grew to enormous heights. As it grew, its lower leaves fell off, leaving a pattern of leaf scars on its bark. Widespread during the Carboniferous Period, Sigillaria died out in the Permian Period.

Lepidodendron
(leh-pi-doh-DEN-dron)

This giant may have reached its full height in just 20 years. Lepidodendron formed enormous tropical forests surrounding watery swamps and had thick rootlike structures to stop it from falling over.

Fact file

» **Height:** 100 ft (30 m)
» **Reproduction:** Cones with spores
» **Period:** Carboniferous
» **Location:** Worldwide

As it grew taller, Lepidodendron's trunk divided into branches.

Most coal is made from the fossilized remains of lycophyte forests.

Lepidodendron fossil

The bark of Lepidodendron had a diamond pattern on it.

Sigillaria's trunk was either unbranched or branched only once.

Sigillaria fossil

The ridges and grooves on the bark of Sigillaria were arranged in vertical lines.

Fact file

» **Height:** 165 ft (50 m)
» **Reproduction:** Cones with spores
» **Period:** Carboniferous
» **Location:** Worldwide

21

Tempskya

(temp-SKI-a)

Tempskya was a type of tree fern that probably grew in swamps and was widespread during the Cretaceous Period. More than 20 different species have been identified from their fossilized trunks.

Fact file

» **Height:** 20 ft (6 m)
» **Reproduction:** Spores
» **Period:** Cretaceous
» **Location:** Worldwide

Unlike tree ferns today, which have a crown of leaves on top, Tempskya grew leaves all over.

Fiddlehead

Young fern leaves start out tightly coiled and are called fiddleheads.

Frond

The fiddlehead unfurls to reveal the leaf, called a frond.

Tree ferns

Modern tree ferns are slow-growing plants that are found in tropical forests around the world. Fronds from large tree ferns can reach 6½ ft (2 m) or more in length.

Tree fern

The trunk was made up of around 200 individual stems surrounded by a mass of roots. Each of these "false trunks" could grow to 20 in (50 cm) across.

Magnolia
(mag-NOH-lee-a)

There are around 300 different types of magnolia alive today. The first members of this family appeared during the late Cretaceous Period, about 100 million years ago, and were likely to have been eaten by dinosaurs.

Fact file

» **Height:** 100 ft (30 m)
» **Reproduction:** Flowers
» **Period:** Cretaceous
» **Location:** Worldwide

The southern magnolia has large white flowers and looks very similar to its prehistoric cousins.

The center of the flower is thick and tough. This stops the beetles that pollinate it from causing too much damage as they snack on its pollen.

Some magnolias are small and shrublike, but the southern magnolia can grow into a tree.

Magnolia bud

Furry jacket

Some magnolias make their flower buds for the next year before the winter. During the cold months, the buds are protected inside soft, furry jackets, which keep them warm.

Magnolia flowers are pollinated by beetles. These flowers evolved before bees did.

Animals through time

The first complex animal life emerged more than 500 million years ago. By studying fossils found around the globe, paleontologists are able to understand when different groups of animals appeared and how life continued to evolve.

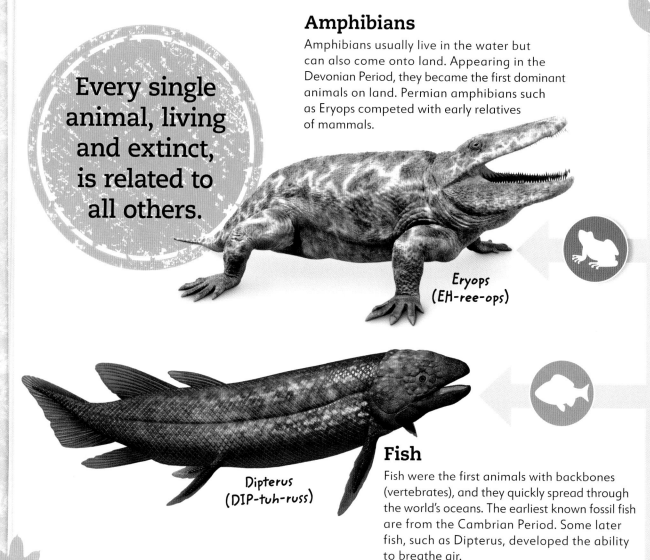

Sinodelphys
(sai-noh-DEL-fiss)

Every single animal, living and extinct, is related to all others.

Amphibians

Amphibians usually live in the water but can also come onto land. Appearing in the Devonian Period, they became the first dominant animals on land. Permian amphibians such as Eryops competed with early relatives of mammals.

Eryops
(EH-ree-ops)

Dipterus
(DIP-tuh-russ)

Fish

Fish were the first animals with backbones (vertebrates), and they quickly spread through the world's oceans. The earliest known fossil fish are from the Cambrian Period. Some later fish, such as Dipterus, developed the ability to breathe air.

Mammals

The first mammals appeared in the Triassic Period, around 225 million years ago, soon after the first dinosaurs. From bats to armadillos and whales to humans, mammals form an incredibly diverse group. Many early mammals, such as Sinodelphys, were small and ratlike.

Diet

Animals that eat only plants are called herbivores, whereas those that eat only meat are called carnivores. When animals eat both plants and meat, they are called omnivores. Carnivores, such as Velociraptor, and herbivores, such as Iguanodon, had different shaped teeth for chewing plants or tearing meat.

Iguanodon teeth

Velociraptor tooth

Birds

More than 150 million years ago, during the Jurassic Period, birds evolved from dinosaurs—and are now the only group of living dinosaurs. Flight allowed giant birds, like Argentavis from the Neogene Period, to take over the skies.

Argentavis
(ar-jen-TAR-viss)

Reptiles

Reptiles evolved from amphibians during the Carboniferous Period. Their waterproof eggs meant that, unlike amphibians, reptiles could live entirely on land. However, some, such as crocodile-like Protosuchus, were also able to swim.

Protosuchus
(proh-toh-SOOK-uss)

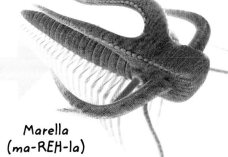

Marella
(ma-REH-la)

Invertebrates

The first animals to evolve were invertebrates. They include many groups, from snails to spiders and worms to corals, but none of them have a bony internal skeleton. Some odd-looking invertebrates, such as Marella, appeared during the Cambrian Period.

Dickinsonia

(dik-in-SOH-nee-a)

Living some 570 million years ago, Dickinsonia is one of the most ancient and mysterious of all animals, although scientists cannot agree exactly what type of animal it is. Several types have been identified, but its life cycle remains a mystery.

» **Length:** 3 ft (1 m)
» **Diet:** Herbivore
» **Period:** First life
» **Location:** Asia, Europe, and Oceania

A triangular segment has been interpreted as Dickinsonia's head by some scientists, although others have suggested it is more likely to be the back end.

The body was disk-shaped and flattened like a pancake.

A midline groove separated multiple segments on either side of the body.

Dickinsonia fossil

Sand print

Dickinsonia had no hard parts, so all fossils are of impressions of it made in sand. The first Dickinsonia fossils were found in the Ediacara Hills in Australia during the 1900s.

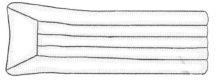

The fluid-filled chambers of this squishy animal were pressurized, a bit like an inflatable mattress!

Hallucigenia

(ha-loo-si-JEE-nee-a)

Hallucigenia is one of the most unusual Cambrian critters ever found. It was a wormlike animal that lived in the sea and had rows of spikes on its back—scientists initially thought the spines were its legs!

» **Length:** 2 in (5 cm)
» **Diet:** Carnivore
» **Period:** Cambrian
» **Location:** Asia and North America

Multiple rows of thin spiked spines ran along its back and may have been used for protection.

Hallucigenia had a small head with two primitive eyes, a mouth, and a throat containing tiny needlelike teeth.

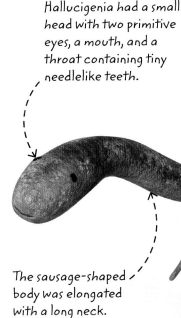

The sausage-shaped body was elongated with a long neck.

Seven pairs of legs ended in tiny claws, but three pairs of clawless arms were found at the front.

Velvet worms

Paleontologists have shown that Hallucigenia may be a member of a group of animals that include modern-day velvet worms. These animals live on the land and also move using clawed feet.

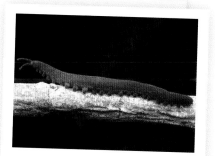

Velvet worm

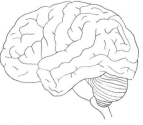

Hallucigenia's odd shape inspired its name, which means "wandering of the mind."

Paraceraurus

(pa-ra-seh-ROR-uss)

Paraceraurus was a type of trilobite. This group of marine invertebrates was among the most successful early animals, but it disappeared during the extinction event at the end of the Permian Period. More than 20,000 different trilobites have been discovered.

Paraceraurus had antennae that it used to sense its environment.

Long spiny appendages were possibly used for defense against predators or perhaps as sensory organs.

A shieldlike segmented body helped to protect trilobites from predators. Many were capable of rolling into an armadillo-like ball.

It can take hundreds of hours to clean a delicate trilobite fossil.

Burgess Shale

The Burgess Shale in Canada is one of the most important fossil sites in the world. Many types of fossil are preserved in the rocks, which are roughly 510 million years old, including many trilobites.

Burgess Shale, Canada

Anomalocaris

(a-nom-a-loh-KAR-iss)

Anomalocaris was a giant in the Cambrian oceans and one of the world's first super predators, grabbing prey with its large mouthparts. The very first fossils belonging to this early shrimplike invertebrate were found in the famous Burgess Shale.

Fact file

» **Length:** 3 ft (1 m)
» **Diet:** Carnivore
» **Period:** Cambrian
» **Location:** Asia, North America, and Oceania

A pair of huge eyes were set on stalks on each side of its head.

Two large grasping appendages were used to shuffle prey into its circular mouth.

Anomalocaris's body was made up of multiple segments. Instead of legs, it had flaps along its sides, which helped it to swim.

Cambrian Explosion

The "Cambrian Explosion" refers to the rapid expansion of different life-forms in the Cambrian Period. Lots of weird and wonderful new animals appeared, including species such as Anomalocaris and the bizarre Wiwaxia (wi-WAKS-ee-a).

Wiwaxia

Anomalocaris had excellent vision. Like an insect, it had compound eyes that contained thousands of small lenses.

29

Heliophyllum

(hee-lee-oh-FAI-lum)

Heliophyllum is an extinct type of coral nicknamed a "horn coral," after the hornlike shape of its fossils. It added one thin ridge to its rocky skeleton every day—about 400 a year—as the Earth turned more quickly in the Devonian Period, and a year had more days.

Long tentacles, possibly containing stinging cells, helped to catch tiny prey as they drifted past the coral.

Heliophyllum fossils are very common and are often found together in large numbers.

Food was passed into the mouth by the tentacles. Waste was also expelled from the mouth.

The pointed end of Heliophyllum's rocky skeleton would have been anchored to the seafloor.

Coral reef

Heliophyllum lived alone, but many corals grow together to create coral reefs. Reefs form important habitats that support thousands of species, including fish, crustaceans, and mollusks, such as octopuses and snails.

Coral reef

Encrinus

(en-KRY-nuss)

Although it may have looked a little bit like a plant, Encrinus was a type of marine animal called a crinoid, which are related to starfish and sea urchins. Crinoids with long stems attached to the seafloor are known as "sea lilies" due to their flowerlike appearance.

The long stem of sea lilies is made up of lots of tiny segments called ossicles, which are commonly found as fossils.

Encrinus's cuplike head, called a calyx, had 10 feathery arms, which it used to filter small prey from the water.

Encrinus fossils are usually found with their arms closed together.

At the base of the long stem was a rootlike anchor, called a holdfast, which attached Encrinus to the seafloor.

Crinoid cousins

The oldest fossil crinoids are around 485 million years old, and thousands of fossil species have been identified. Today, there are around 600 species that live in the oceans. Some species are capable of walking along the seabed!

Sea lily today

31

Eurypterus

(yoo-RIP-teh-russ)

Named in 1825, Eurypterus gives its name to a group of extinct invertebrates called eurypterids—commonly nicknamed "sea scorpions." These top predators swam in prehistoric seas searching for trilobites and fish to eat.

Fact file

» **Length:** 4 ft (1.3 m)
» **Diet:** Carnivore
» **Period:** Silurian
» **Location:** Europe and North America

One type of Eurypterus is the state fossil of New York.

Eurypterus pushed itself through the water with large paddlelike legs. They possibly helped it crawl on land as well.

The long spikelike tail spine, called a telson, may have been used as a weapon.

Sea scorpions

More than 200 species of eurypterid have been found. The largest was Jaekelopterus (yay-kel-OP-teh-russ). At 9 ft (2.6 m) long, it was the biggest arthropod of all time and it had fearsome spiked pincers.

Jaekelopterus

The front limbs were used for walking and holding prey while feeding.

Although eurypterids look like scorpions, their tail spine wasn't venomous like a scorpion's stinger.

Mesolimulus

(mez-oh-LIM-yoo-luss)

Mesolimulus is an extinct type of horseshoe crab whose fossils are most commonly found in the Jurassic rocks of Solnhofen in southern Germany. It is so similar to the living horseshoe crab Limulus, that it was once thought to be the same animal.

» **Length:** 20 in (50 cm)
» **Diet:** Carnivore
» **Period:** Jurassic
» **Location:** Europe, Africa, and Asia

A rounded shieldlike shell protected the body and hid its 10 legs, which it used to walk around the seafloor.

The telson, a spinelike tail, helped Mesolimulus turn over if it was flipped upside down.

Like living species, Mesolimulus probably had 10 eyes! Two were large and the other eight were very small.

This 32-ft (9.7-m) track was created by Mesolimulus. We know this because its fossil was found at the end of the track!

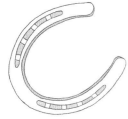

Horseshoe crabs get their common name from their horseshoelike shape.

Horseshoe crab

Horseshoe crabs

Despite their name, horseshoe crabs are not crabs at all. They are a group of invertebrates more closely related to spiders and eurypterids than to crabs. The oldest examples of horseshoe crabs are about 450 million years old.

Scaphites

(skaf-AI-teez)

Fact file

» **Length:** 8 in (20 cm) shell
» **Diet:** Carnivore
» **Period:** Cretaceous
» **Location:** Worldwide

With their distinctive spiral shells, ammonites are among the most common fossils. These sea animals were related to octopuses and ranged in size from as small as coins to as huge as tractor tires. Scaphites was one of the last—all ammonites became extinct soon after the Cretaceous asteroid.

This Hoplites ammonite fossil seems to be cast in gold—but it's actually made of the mineral pyrite.

Ammonites probably had between 8 and 10 arms.

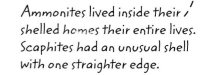

Two long feeding tentacles were used to grab prey.

Ammonites lived inside their shelled homes their entire lives. Scaphites had an unusual shell with one straighter edge.

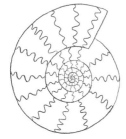

Some ammonite fossils have wiggly lines on them called sutures.

Nautiluses

The modern nautilus (NAW-ti-luss) resembles an ammonite. Like ammonites, nautiluses have chambers in their shells that can be filled with either water or gas to help them float or sink.

Nautilus

Cylindroteuthis

(si-lin-dro-TOO-thiss)

Squidlike Cylindroteuthis was a belemnite. Belemnites are known mostly for their bullet-shaped fossils—remains of the animal's internal skeleton, called a guard. Rare fossils show their soft parts, including their arms and ink sac. Some artists have even used the fossilized ink to paint with!

Large eyes and good vision meant Cylindroteuthis could hunt in the dark.

It was once believed that belemnite fossils were created by lightning bolts striking the ground.

Winglike fins helped to make Cylindroteuthis a powerful swimmer.

Belemnites had 10 arms with hundreds of tiny hooks on them that were used to catch prey.

The fossilized guard of a belemnite is also called a rostrum.

Squid pen

Squid are closely related to belemnites and also have an internal skeleton—called a pen. The ancestors of squid had shells, but these have become the internal pens over millions of years.

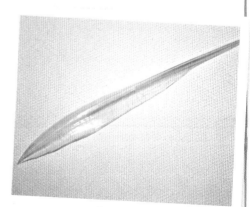

Squid pen

Arthropleura

(arth-ro-PLOO-ra)

Longer than most people are tall, Arthropleura was a truly enormous millipede. As it grew, it repeatedly shed its hard outer skeleton so it could get longer and grow new pairs of legs.

» **Length:** 8 ft (2.5 m)
» **Diet:** Herbivore
» **Period:** Carboniferous
» **Location:** Europe and North America

Arthropleura used antennae to sense and feel its way around the dark, damp forest floor.

LARGEST INVERTEBRATE EVER TO LIVE ON LAND

Some Arthropleura fossils have been discovered with plant remains inside their bellies.

Its body had up to 30 segments that each had two pairs of legs attached—making around 120 legs in total.

Millipedes

There are many types of millipede living today, but the largest can only grow to 16 in (40 cm) long. Although the word millipede means "a thousand feet," all have fewer legs than this.

African giant millipede

Fossilized Arthropleura tracks show that its legs were about 20 in (50 cm) apart.

Meganeura
(meh-ga-NYOO-ra)

Long before pterosaurs, birds, or bats, insects were the first animals to evolve flight. The largest of all these flying insects were the griffin flies, such as Meganeura, which lived some 300 million years ago.

» **Wingspan:** 30 in (75 cm)
» **Diet:** Carnivore
» **Period:** Carboniferous
» **Location:** Europe

Dragonflies

Modern-day dragonflies are cousins of the mighty griffin flies, but they don't grow nearly as big. The higher levels of oxygen in the Carboniferous Period may have helped prehistoric insects reach super-big sizes.

Emperor dragonfly

Using its four wings, Meganeura could fly quickly, snatching its prey in midair.

Meganeura had large eyes and powerful jaws. It was a top hunter, feeding on other insects and perhaps even small amphibians and fish.

Small but strong spines on its legs were used to hold struggling prey in place, so it could deliver a deadly bite.

Fossils show that Meganeura had a wingspan as wide as that of the common kestrel.

37

Dunkleosteus

(dun-KEL-oss-tee-uss)

This armored giant belonged to an extinct group of fish called placoderms. Dunkleosteus appeared toward the end of the Devonian Period and had one of the most powerful bites of any animal ever. It feasted on whatever it could catch.

Fact file

» **Length:** 33 ft (10 m)
» **Diet:** Carnivore
» **Period:** Devonian
» **Location:** Africa, Europe, and North America

Dunkleosteus's enormous head and the front half of its body were protected by thick armor plating.

Large fins suggest that Dunkleosteus was able to change direction quickly and efficiently.

Instead of teeth, Dunkleosteus had self-sharpening, fanglike bony plates that were capable of slicing prey in half.

On the menu

Some Dunkleosteus fossils have been found with bite marks matching the jaws of other Dunkleosteus. This suggests that they may have been cannibals, occasionally eating their own kind.

Dunkleosteus was the largest predator of its day.

Cephalaspis

(ke-fa-LASP-iss)

Cephalaspis was a type of jawless fish. Instead of biting and chewing its food, Cephalaspis used its muscular mouth to suck up prey, such as crustaceans and worms, which it searched for on the muddy seafloor.

Fact file

» **Length:** 10 in (25 cm)
» **Diet:** Carnivore
» **Period:** Devonian
» **Location:** Europe
   and North America

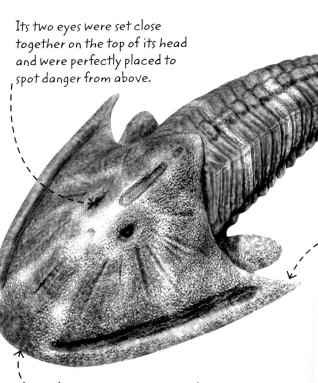

Its two eyes were set close together on the top of its head and were perfectly placed to spot danger from above.

The spikelike projections at the back of its head are called "cornua." Cephalaspis may have used them to dig for food.

A huge horseshoe-shaped shield protected its head.

Lampreys

Cephalaspis was a member of an extinct group of armored jawless fish called ostracoderms. The only living jawless fish are lampreys and hagfish. They have rows of teeth to clamp onto prey.

Many complete Cephalaspis fossils have been discovered. They were first studied in 1835.

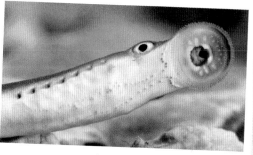

Lamprey

Helicoprion

(hel-i-ko-PRY-on)

Helicoprion was an unusual sharklike fish whose name means "spiral saw." Almost all known Helicoprion fossils are of its spiral-shaped cluster of teeth, called a tooth whorl. The largest whorls may have been more than 24 in (60 cm) long.

- » **Length:** 33 ft (10 m)
- » **Diet:** Carnivore
- » **Period:** Permian
- » **Location:** Worldwide

The tooth whorls resembled the blades on a chainsaw.

A large powerful tail helped it move swiftly through the water.

Helicoprion probably had a streamlined body that was well suited for moving fast when chasing prey.

Like most modern-day sharks, Helicoprion may have had five pairs of gill slits.

The tooth whorl was set into the lower jaw and was used to slice up prey.

This fossil whorl shows the older smaller teeth, which were pushed into its center as new larger teeth formed on the outside.

Ratfish relative

The body of Helicoprion was made of soft cartilage, so fossilized remains are rare. However, some known fossils show that its closest living relatives are the chimaeras—also known as ratfish.

Chimaera

Megalodon

(MEH-ga-lo-don)

The mighty mega-toothed megalodon, scientific name Otodus, was a shark of giant proportions. Paleontologists have shown that it had the strongest bite force of any animal ever—three times stronger than a Tyrannosaurus!

» **Length:** 60 ft (18 m)
» **Diet:** Carnivore
» **Period:** Neogene
» **Location:** Worldwide

LARGEST SHARK EVER TO LIVE

Thick, strong serrated teeth were ideal for slicing through flesh. A megalodon's teeth were constantly replaced throughout its life.

Great white sharks

Megalodons resembled great white sharks in appearance and lifestyle, and the two species actually lived at the same time. It is possible that great white sharks fought young megalodons for food and this could have played a part in the megalodon's extinction.

Large pectoral fins were used for balance and helped it to change direction while swimming.

Megalodons had huge teeth—the largest found are about 7 in (18 cm) long, as long as an adult human hand!

Great white shark

41

From water to land

In a crowded underwater world full of competition, making the move onto land provided a way to escape from predators, explore new environments, and take advantage of new sources of food. This is exactly what early amphibians did around 380 million years ago.

Many animals, including whales, returned to the water from land.

Eusthenopteron

Tiktaalik

Animal explorers

Fish with limblike fins, such as Eusthenopteron and Tiktaalik, evolved into the first vertebrates with four legs, called tetrapods. These new tetrapods probably first crawled out of freshwater swamps, but they returned to the water to lay their eggs.

Stepping onto land

During the Devonian Period, the first fish with limblike fins evolved. Over the course of millions of years, the bones in their fins became better developed for taking the first steps on land.

Eusthenopteron
(yoos-theh-NOP-te-ron)

Tiktaalik
(tik-TAH-lik)

In the water
Some prehistoric fish, such as Eusthenopteron, had bones that resembled those of early tetrapods and lungs to breathe air.

Part in water
Not yet capable of walking on land, species such as Tiktaalik had limblike fins that helped them to drag their bodies around swamps.

Plant groundbreakers

Plants developed various features that helped them to switch to a life on land. A waxy outer layer, called a cuticle, prevented them from drying out, and strong stems let them grow upright.

Cooksonia

Lungfish

Modern lungfish have lungs as well as gills, which allow them to breathe air when oxygen levels in the water are too low. The ability to breathe air was an essential skill for the first land-living tetrapods.

Australian lungfish

Tiktaalik had a well-developed tailfin that helped it to swim.

Acanthostega
(ah-kan-tho-STEE-gah)

Eryops
(EH-ree-ops)

Out of water
Like their fish ancestors, tetrapods such as Acanthostega still spent most of their time in water, but their feet show that they were able to walk.

Amphibian
Capable of living comfortably both in and out of water, the first amphibians—such as Eryops—gained a firm foothold on land and became the dominant predators.

Tiktaalik

(tik-TAH-lik)

It may have crawled out of the water like an amphibian, but Tiktaalik was actually a fish! It belonged to a group known as lobe-finned fish, which have limblike fins, and Tiktaalik fossils have helped scientists to better understand how four-legged land animals evolved.

Fact file

» **Length:** 10 ft (3 m)
» **Diet:** Carnivore
» **Period:** Devonian
» **Location:** North America

The coelacanth is a living example of a lobe-finned fish.

A sturdy, well-developed rib cage helped to support the weight of Tiktaalik when it came out of the water and onto the land.

Behind its eyes were two openings called "spiracles," which suggest Tiktaalik had simple lungs as well as gills.

Armlike, bony front fins with powerful muscles helped Tiktaalik to push and pull its body along the ground.

Panderichthys

Panderichthys (pan-der-IK-thiss) was another ancient lobe-finned fish, but it lived only in water. Because of their mix of fish and tetrapod (animals with four limbs) features, they are sometimes called "fishapods."

Panderichthys

The first Tiktaalik fossils were unearthed in 2004.

Metoposaurus

(meh-to-po-SOR-uss)

Metoposaurus was a primitive type of salamander-like amphibian that grew as big as a car and was a top predator. Catching prey in the water and on land, it had a similar lifestyle to a crocodile.

A large broad tail moved from side to side when swimming and propelled Metoposaurus through the water.

Its limbs were small and weak. This would have made movement on land rather clumsy, so Metoposaurus could only have crawled for short periods.

Amphibamus

Another primitive amphibian, newt-sized Amphibamus (am-fee-BAH-muss) lived during the Carboniferous Period, when it inhabited lush tropical swamps. Amphibamus may have been a close ancestor of modern amphibians.

Amphibamus

Metoposaurus had hundreds of sharp teeth, which it used to snap up fish and other animals.

Dimetrodon

(dai-MET-roh-don)

Dimetrodon was the world's first truly big land predator and is often mistaken for a dinosaur due to its appearance. However, it lived long before the dinosaurs and was actually part of a group of animals that were more closely related to mammals than reptiles.

» **Length:** 11 ft (3.5 m)
» **Diet:** Carnivore
» **Period:** Permian
» **Location:** Europe and North America

An enormous sail may have been used for display or to help control Dimetrodon's temperature. It was held up by long bones.

Large canine teeth at the front helped to tear up chunks of meat.

Strong jaw muscles attached through the single hole behind the eye socket. The same feature is also found in humans.

Dimetrodon's sprawling legs held its belly and tail off the ground.

Similar sail

Another sail-backed animal related to Dimetrodon was the herbivorous Edaphosaurus (ed-A-fo-sor-uss). However, its sail had lots of spikelike bony projections sticking out of it.

Edaphosaurus

Varanus priscus

(VA-ra-nuss PRIS-kuss)

Varanus priscus, previously called Megalania, was a gigantic monitor lizard that reached twice the size of today's largest living lizard—the Komodo dragon. It is believed that early humans may have driven this giant lizard to extinction.

Fact file

» **Length:** 23 ft (7 m)
» **Diet:** Carnivore
» **Period:** Quaternary
» **Location:** Australia

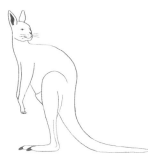

Giant prehistoric kangaroos, such as Procoptodon (proh-KOP-to-don), were probably on Varanus's menu.

Varanus's teeth were curved and had sharp cutting edges ideal for biting through flesh.

LARGEST LIZARD EVER TO LIVE

Its legs pointed outward and it may have walked with a side-to-side motion like modern lizards.

Varanus had scaly skin that may have been patterned.

Fossil Varanus vertebrae—parts of the backbone—can be used to estimate how big Varanus grew.

Komodo dragons

Studies of the skull and teeth of Varanus show that it may have delivered a venomous bite, just like modern Komodo dragons. This makes Varanus the largest venomous vertebrate known.

Komodo dragon

Ichthyosaurs

(IK-thee-uh-sors)

Ichthyosaurs were a remarkable group of air-breathing marine reptiles that appeared in the Triassic Period. Many resembled dolphins, but they evolved into a wide range of different species, including the first sea animals to reach truly gigantic sizes.

Ophthalmosaurus had enormous eyes the size of dinner plates. Its excellent vision helped it hunt prey in deep, dark waters.

Shonisaurus
(sho-nee-SOR-uss)

Shonisaurus was a massive ichthyosaur—three times the length of a killer whale. However, jawbones from another ichthyosaur found in the UK hint at a bigger animal the size of a blue whale.

Fact file

» **Length:** 69 ft (21 m)
» **Diet:** Carnivore
» **Period:** Triassic
» **Location:** North America

Shonisaurus had a deeper body than most ichthyosaurs and probably lacked a dorsal fin.

Fact file

» **Length:** 6$\frac{1}{2}$ ft (2 m)
» **Diet:** Carnivore
» **Period:** Triassic
» **Location:** Asia, Europe, and North America

Mixosaurus
(mik-so-SOR-uss)

Mixosaurus was one of the earliest ichthyosaurs to appear and it is the most common Triassic ichthyosaur known. It chased down fish to eat, steering with its flipperlike limbs.

Unlike later ichthyosaurs, Mixosaurus did not have a crescent-shaped tail.

Its jaws contained hundreds of sharp, pointed teeth that were ideal for catching slippery prey.

Fact file

» **Length:** 16 ft (5 m)
» **Diet:** Carnivore
» **Period:** Jurassic
» **Location:** Europe
and North America

Ophthalmosaurus
(op-thal-mo-SOR-uss)

Like many of the later ichthyosaurs, Ophthalmosaurus had a typical dolphin-shaped body that was perfectly suited for chasing fish and squid at high speeds through the water.

Stenopterygius had a curved tail fin that it beat from side to side to propel itself forward.

LARGEST
SEA REPTILE
EVER TO LIVE

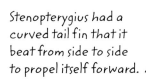

Stenopterygius
(steh-nop-tuh-RI-jee-uss)

Thousands of Stenopterygius fossils have been discovered—mostly in quarries near the town of Holzmaden, Germany. This powerful reptile could swim at speeds of around 45 mph (70 kph)!

Fact file

» **Length:** 16 ft (5 m)
» **Diet:** Carnivore
» **Period:** Jurassic
» **Location:** Europe

Ichthyosaurus
(ik-thee-uh-SOR-uss)

Ichthyosaurus was the first ichthyosaur to be named. Many early finds were discovered by paleontologist Mary Anning. Fossils show that Ichthyosaurus, like other ichthyosaurs, gave birth to live young rather than laying eggs.

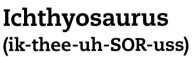

Fact file

» **Length:** 10 ft (3 m)
» **Diet:** Carnivore
» **Period:** Jurassic
» **Location:** Europe
and North America

Mosasaurus

(moh-za-SOR-uss)

The first Mosasaurus fossil found was a huge skull unearthed deep inside a quarry in the Netherlands during the late 1700s. Mosasaurus belonged to a group of marine lizards called mosasaurs. They had flippers for limbs and were deadly hunters in prehistoric seas.

Fact file

» **Length:** 50 ft (15 m)
» **Diet:** Carnivore
» **Period:** Cretaceous
» **Location:** Africa, Europe, and North America

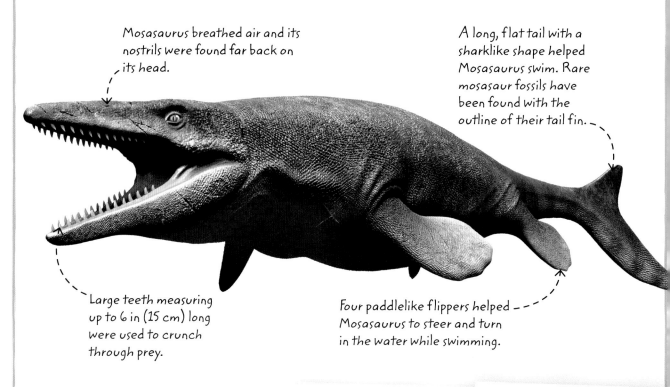

Mosasaurus breathed air and its nostrils were found far back on its head.

A long, flat tail with a sharklike shape helped Mosasaurus swim. Rare mosasaur fossils have been found with the outline of their tail fin.

Large teeth measuring up to 6 in (15 cm) long were used to crunch through prey.

Four paddlelike flippers helped Mosasaurus to steer and turn in the water while swimming.

Mosasaurus's skull shows its rows of sharp teeth and strong jaws.

Light bite

Many ammonite shells with bite marks matching the teeth of mosasaurs have been discovered. Mosasaurs had conical teeth that left round puncture holes, such as those seen here.

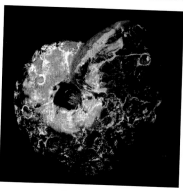

Ammonite

Zarafasaura

(za-ra-fuh-SOR-a)

Zarafasaura belonged to a group of reptiles called elasmosaurs, a type of plesiosaur. They had very long necks and swam in the ocean, however, as reptiles they had to come to the surface to breathe. Fossils of Zarafasaura have been found in Morocco.

Long, slender teeth were perfectly adapted for catching fish.

Some elasmosaurs had more than 70 vertebrae in their neck, whereas humans have only seven! Zarafasaura may have had up to 60.

Only two Zarafasaura skulls have been found. This fossil was carefully reconstructed from a skull that was crushed.

Zarafasaura means "giraffe lizard."

Four large flippers were used to "fly" through the water.

Pliosaurs

Although pliosaurs looked like mosasaurs, they were more closely related to elasmosaurs. Species such as Liopleurodon (lai-oh-PLOO-ro-don) were top ocean predators. One pliosaur discovered even had the remains of a dinosaur inside its stomach.

Liopleurodon

Deinosuchus

(dai-no-SOO-kuss)

This supersized relative of the alligator was one of the deadliest predators alive during the late Cretaceous Period. It might be the largest crocodilian that ever lived, rivaled only by the huge Sarcosuchus from Africa and South America.

» **Length:** 33 ft (10 m)
» **Diet:** Carnivore
» **Period:** Cretaceous
» **Location:** North America

With just its snout and eyes poking out of the water, Deinosuchus carefully stalked its prey.

Powerful jaws with large conical teeth were used to inflict bone-crushing bites and tear chunks of flesh from prey.

A strong, muscular tail helped Deinosuchus to swim through the water and lunge at prey.

The largest living crocodilian is the saltwater crocodile, which can grow up to 20 ft (6 m).

Deinosuchus used its short limbs to drag itself onto riverbanks.

Ambush hunting

Lying underwater, waiting for the perfect moment to strike, Deinosuchus would have been an expert ambush predator. It hunted a variety of animals, including dinosaurs, and probably drowned its prey before eating it.

Deinosuchus attacking Albertosaurus

Titanoboa

(tai-tan-oh-BOH-a)

At more than three times the length of an average green anaconda—one of the largest snakes alive today—Titanoboa was a prehistoric giant. All the fossils of this snake have been discovered in a coal mine in Columbia.

» **Length:** 46 ft (14 m)
» **Diet:** Carnivore
» **Period:** Paleogene
» **Location:** South America

LARGEST SNAKE EVER TO LIVE

Sharp, backward-facing teeth were used to hold Titanoboa's prey tight, while flexible jaws opened to swallow it whole.

Titanoboa was up to 3 ft (1 m) wide!

Titanoboa was a constrictor snake that squeezed its prey to death. This super serpent probably preyed on large fish, turtles, and crocodiles.

Titanoboa lived about 60 million years ago in tropical swamps and forests, similar to today's Amazon Rain Forest.

Robotic Titanoboa

A team of artists and engineers created a life-sized robotic Titanoboa that was modeled on fossils of the real snake. It shows how Titanoboa might have moved.

Pterosaurs

(TEH-ruh-sors)

Pterosaurs were a bizarre and fascinating group of reptiles that were the first vertebrate animals to evolve flight. They flew on batlike wings that stretched from their fingers to their legs. The earliest pterosaurs appeared during the Triassic.

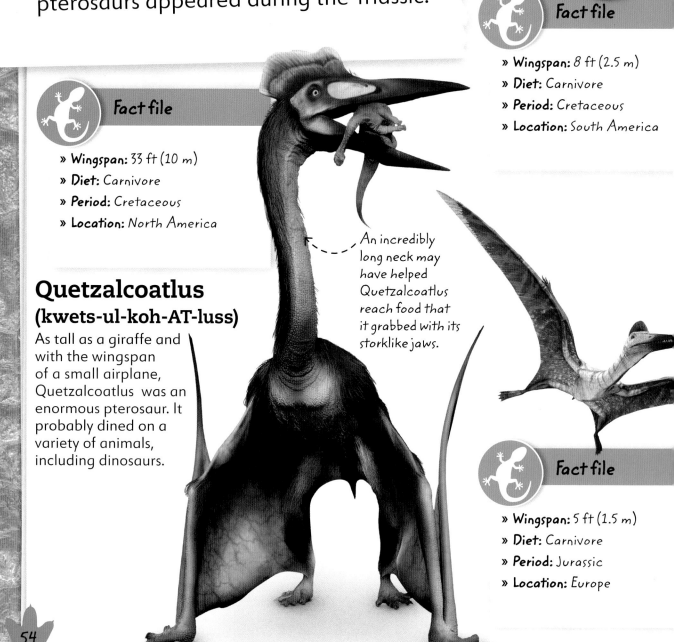

Fact file

> » **Wingspan:** 8 ft (2.5 m)
> » **Diet:** Carnivore
> » **Period:** Cretaceous
> » **Location:** South America

Fact file

> » **Wingspan:** 33 ft (10 m)
> » **Diet:** Carnivore
> » **Period:** Cretaceous
> » **Location:** North America

Quetzalcoatlus
(kwets-ul-koh-AT-luss)

As tall as a giraffe and with the wingspan of a small airplane, Quetzalcoatlus was an enormous pterosaur. It probably dined on a variety of animals, including dinosaurs.

An incredibly long neck may have helped Quetzalcoatlus reach food that it grabbed with its storklike jaws.

Fact file

> » **Wingspan:** 5 ft (1.5 m)
> » **Diet:** Carnivore
> » **Period:** Jurassic
> » **Location:** Europe

Many pterosaurs, such as Tupandactylus, had elaborate head crests.

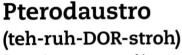

Its jaws were packed with hundreds of needlelike teeth.

Pterodaustro
(teh-ruh-DOR-stroh)

Pterodaustro was a filter feeder that used its long, curved bill to filter small animals from water between its teeth. It hunted in shallow water and had webbed feet for walking on wet ground.

Fact file

» **Wingspan:** 10 ft (3 m)
» **Diet:** Carnivore
» **Period:** Cretaceous
» **Location:** South America

Tupandactylus
(too-pan-DAK-ti-luss)

Tupandactylus had the largest crest of any known pterosaur. This was probably brightly colored and used for display. All of its fossils have been found in Brazil.

Some rare Pterodactylus fossils preserve the shape of its thin wings.

Fact file

» **Wingspan:** 2 m (6 ft)
» **Diet:** Carnivore
» **Period:** Jurassic
» **Location:** Europe

A very long tail ended with a triangular-shaped vane that acted as a rudder to help steer during flight.

Pterodactylus
(teh-ruh-DAK-ti-luss)

The first pterosaur to be discovered was Pterodactylus, and some people call this group of animals pterodactyls. When it landed, its wings folded back so it could walk on its hands and feet.

Rhamphorhynchus
(ram-fo-RINK-uss)

More than 100 Rhamphorhynchus fossils have been discovered and this makes it the best-known pterosaur. Some have been found with their last meal of fish preserved inside their guts.

What is a dinosaur?

Dinosaurs were an extraordinary group of reptiles that ruled the world during the Mesozoic Era. Although similar to some other reptiles, their skeletons were different in certain ways, and a dinosaur's legs were held directly beneath its body.

Dreadnoughtus
(dred-NOT-uss)

As reptiles, all dinosaurs had a covering of tough scales, although we now know many also had feathers.

Dinosaurs held their legs directly beneath their bodies. Dreadnoughtus had columnlike legs to support its huge weight.

Dinosaurs

There were many different types of dinosaur, from ferocious theropod Tyrannosaurus to the gigantic sauropod Dreadnoughtus. However, all dinosaurs shared some similar features, even though they looked very different.

Types of dinosaur

The dinosaur family can be divided into two groups: the Saurischia, which have lizardlike hips, and the Ornithischia, which have birdlike hips. Confusingly, birds evolved from the lizard-hipped dinosaurs!

Ornithischians

The ornithischians feature familiar dinosaurs, including stegosaurs, such as Stegosaurus, and ankylosaurs, such as Sauropelta.

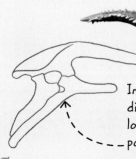

In bird-hipped dinosaurs, both lower hip bones point backward.

Sauropelta
(sor-uh-PEL-ta)

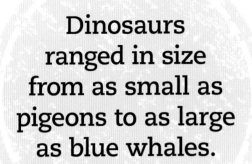

Dinosaurs ranged in size from as small as pigeons to as large as blue whales.

Eggs

Dinosaurs laid hard-shelled eggs, but their shape, size, and color varied. The world's oldest known dinosaur eggs are from a sauropod called Massospondylus (mass-oh-SPON-di-luss), collected from Jurassic rocks in South Africa.

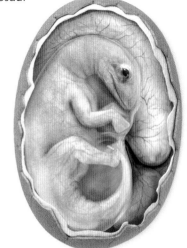

Dinosaur egg

All dinosaurs had claws. Predators had sharp talons, but herbivores often had hooflike nails.

Most dinosaurs used their tails for balance. Dreadnoughtus may have whipped its tail from side to side as a form of defense.

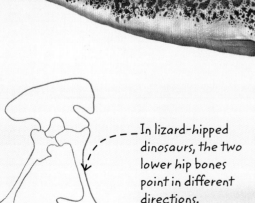

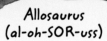

Allosaurus
(al-oh-SOR-uss)

Saurischians

The saurischians include theropods, such as Tyrannosaurus and Allosaurus, and mighty sauropods, such as Diplodocus and Giraffatitan.

In lizard-hipped dinosaurs, the two lower hip bones point in different directions.

Eodromaeus

(ee-oh-dro-MAY-uss)

One of the earliest dinosaurs to have lived, Eodromaeus was among the first theropods—and, like most of them, it ate meat. It was named in 2011 after an almost complete skeleton was found in Argentina.

» **Length:** 3 ft (1 m)
» **Diet:** Carnivore
» **Period:** Triassic
» **Location:** South America

A narrow skull and jaws filled with sharp, curved teeth were designed to chomp on small reptiles.

Eodromaeus had a lightly built skeleton and it is estimated to have weighed around 11 lb (5 kg)—about as heavy as a pet cat.

Long arms with three sharp claws were used to slash at and hold Eodromaeus's prey.

Eodromaeus means "dawn runner."

Long legs gave this small predator an advantage when chasing down prey or escaping from larger predators.

Another early dinosaur, Eoraptor (ee-oh-RAP-tuh), looked like Eodromaeus but may have been more closely related to sauropods.

Herrerasaurus

First dinosaurs

The earliest dinosaurs, like Eodromaeus, Eoraptor, and Herrerasaurus (heh-reh-ra-SOR-uss), lived during the Late Triassic—around 231 million years ago. Fossils of these dinosaurs help paleontologists to better understand how the first dinosaurs evolved.

Stegosaurus

(steh-guh-SOR-uss)

With two rows of tall plates along its back, Stegosaurus is one of the most instantly recognizable dinosaurs. Despite being known from multiple fossils, complete and well-preserved skeletons are very rare.

Stegosaurus had a small head, and a brain about the size of a plum.

Two rows of diamond-shaped bony plates ran along Stegosaurus's neck, back, and tail and were probably used for display.

Protective throat armor has been found on some Stegosaurus fossils.

Four spikes at the end of the tail were used for protection against predators. Stegosaurus swung its tail from side to side as a deadly weapon.

Stegosaurs

These dinosaurs were herbivores with armorlike plates and defensive spikes. The first stegosaurs appeared in the Jurassic, and one of the oldest species is Huayangosaurus (hwah-yang-o-SOR-uss) from China.

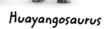

Huayangosaurus

Bones of the meat-eating Allosaurus (al-oh-SOR-uss) have been found with holes matching the points of fossilized Stegosaurus tail spikes, such as this one.

Velociraptor

(veh-loss-i-RAP-tuh)

The speedy Velociraptor belonged to a family of dinosaurs called dromaeosaurs, more commonly known as "raptors." Despite its reputation as a deadly predator, Velociraptor was a small dinosaur, but evidence suggests that it may have hunted in packs.

» **Length:** 6½ ft (2 m)
» **Diet:** Carnivore
» **Period:** Cretaceous
» **Location:** Asia

An extremely long, feathery tail was used for balance when running.

Velociraptor was only about the size of a turkey.

Dromaeosaurs had a curved killing claw on each foot, used to slash and pin down prey.

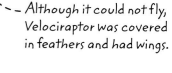

Although it could not fly, Velociraptor was covered in feathers and had wings.

Final fight

One Velociraptor fossil was found attacking another dinosaur, called Protoceratops (proh-toh-SEH-ra-tops), a smaller relative of Triceratops. The herbivore had fought back, though—it was found biting the Velociraptor's arm!

Protoceratops

Fossilized toe-claws like this one have been collected from the Gobi Desert in Mongolia.

Deinocheirus

(dai-no-KAI-russ)

The first fossils of Deinocheirus were discovered in 1965 when paleontologists found a pair of enormous arms with huge claws in the Gobi Desert in Mongolia. This bizarre humpbacked dinosaur was related to meat-eaters, but it ate plants.

» **Length:** 36 ft (11 m)
» **Diet:** Herbivore
» **Period:** Cretaceous
» **Location:** Asia

Deinocheirus had a long skull with a rounded toothless beak, similar to a duck's bill.

A large humplike sail made Deinocheirus appear bigger and more intimidating, which may have stopped predators from attacking it.

Stomach stones called "gastroliths" have been found inside Deinocheirus fossils. These helped it to grind up and digest plants.

The tip of its tail may have ended in a feathery fan that could have been used for display and to attract mates.

Very long arms with three blunt, curved claws were used to gather plants and acted as defensive weapons against predators.

Deinocheirus means "terrible hand," named for its enormous clawed arms that were 8 ft (2.5 m) long.

Ostrich mimics

Deinocheirus was the largest member of a group of Cretaceous dinosaurs called ornithomimosaurs, meaning "ostrich mimics." They were omnivorous or herbivorous and some species, such as Struthiomimus (stroo-thee-oh-MAI-muss), were among the fastest of all dinosaurs.

Struthiomimus

Iguanodon

(ig-WAH-nuh-don)

Iguanodon was the second dinosaur ever to be identified. It was named in 1825 after the discovery of several teeth found in a quarry in the UK. This dinosaur lived in large herds, chomping on plants with its hard beak and teeth.

Fact file

» **Length:** 39 ft (12 m)
» **Diet:** Herbivore
» **Period:** Cretaceous
» **Location:** Europe

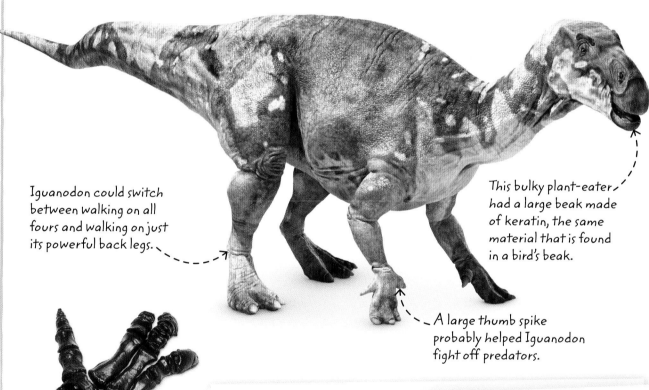

Iguanodon could switch between walking on all fours and walking on just its powerful back legs.

This bulky plant-eater had a large beak made of keratin, the same material that is found in a bird's beak.

A large thumb spike probably helped Iguanodon fight off predators.

The thumb spike can be seen here on the right. It may have been used to help gather plants while feeding, as well as for defense.

Rhino dino

The first Iguanodon fossils discovered were a handful of bones and teeth. Without a complete skeleton, paleontologists thought the thumb spike sat at the end of the nose, a bit like a rhinoceros horn.

Early Iguanodon sculptures in Crystal Palace Park in London, UK

Parasaurolophus

(pa-ra-sor-uh-LOH-fuss)

With its long bony crest, Parasaurolophus is one of the most easily recognizable dinosaurs. A high school student in Utah discovered a nearly complete baby Parasaurolophus fossil that showed the crest was much smaller in young dinosaurs.

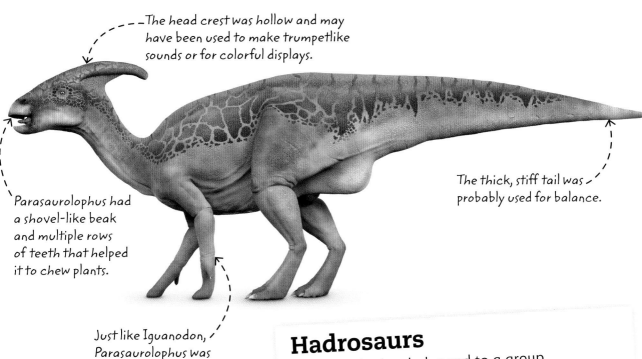

The head crest was hollow and may have been used to make trumpetlike sounds or for colorful displays.

Parasaurolophus had a shovel-like beak and multiple rows of teeth that helped it to chew plants.

The thick, stiff tail was probably used for balance.

Just like Iguanodon, Parasaurolophus was able to walk on all fours as well as on two legs.

Hadrosaurs

Parasaurolophus belonged to a group of dinosaurs called hadrosaurs. Many hadrosaurs, such as Lambeosaurus (lam-bee-oh-SOR-uss), had oddly shaped head crests that may have been brightly colored to attract mates.

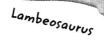

Lambeosaurus

Parasaurolophus's bony crest was part of the skull and there may have been a flap of skin connecting it to the neck.

Sauropods

(SOR-uh-pods)

With their long necks and long tails, the herbivorous sauropods were among the biggest of all the dinosaurs. They include the largest and heaviest animals ever to walk on Earth.

Fact file

» **Length:** 85 ft (26 m)
» **Diet:** Herbivore
» **Period:** Jurassic
» **Location:** Asia

Fact file

» **Length:** 33 ft (10 m)
» **Diet:** Herbivore
» **Period:** Cretaceous
» **Location:** South America

Amargasaurus

(a-mar-ga-SOR-uss)

Amargasaurus was quite small for a sauropod, but it still weighed as much as a rhinoceros. Unusually, it had two rows of tall spines along its neck and back.

Amargasaurus's long spines were likely for display and defense.

Diplodocus

(dip-LOD-o-kuss)

Diplodocus is one of the longest dinosaurs to have existed. The first fossils were discovered in Colorado in 1877. It lived in open woodlands.

Long peglike teeth at the front of Diplodocus's mouth were used like a rake to strip leaves from branches.

Fact file

» **Length:** 85 ft (26 m)
» **Diet:** Herbivore
» **Period:** Jurassic
» **Location:** North America

An extremely long tail made for a deadly whiplike weapon that Diplodocus used to defend itself from hungry predators.

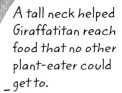

Like other sauropods, Mamenchisaurus had pockets of air inside its neck bones, which made them lighter.

Mamenchisaurus
(ma-men-chee-SOR-uss)

Paleontologists have identified many different species of Mamenchisaurus. One had the longest neck of any animal, spanning almost half its body length.

Fact file

» **Length:** 72 ft (22 m)
» **Diet:** Herbivore
» **Period:** Jurassic
» **Location:** Africa

A tall neck helped Giraffatitan reach food that no other plant-eater could get to.

Giraffatitan
(ji-raf-a-TAI-tan)

At 39 ft (12 m) tall, Giraffatitan towered over most dinosaurs and is one of the tallest ever to have lived. In addition to having a long neck, it had tall front limbs.

Argentinosaurus
(ar-jen-tee-no-SOR-uss)

Heavier than 12 adult elephants, Argentinosaurus was the ultimate heavyweight herbivore. Although many large sauropods have been discovered, paleontologists still consider Argentinosaurus to be the largest.

LARGEST ANIMAL EVER TO LIVE ON LAND

Fact file

» **Length:** 115 ft (35 m)
» **Diet:** Herbivore
» **Period:** Cretaceous
» **Location:** South America

Borealopelta

(bor-ee-al-oh-PEL-ta)

In 2011, one of the best-preserved armored dinosaurs ever discovered was unearthed by miners in Alberta, Canada. It was named Borealopelta. The fossil is so well preserved that it almost looks as if it is sleeping!

Fact file

» **Length:** 18 ft (5.5 m)
» **Diet:** Herbivore
» **Period:** Cretaceous
» **Location:** North America

Rows of bony armor plates covered Borealopelta's body and made it nearly impossible for predators to bite it.

Fragments of skin tell us that Borealopelta was reddish-brown on top and lighter underneath.

A pair of long, menacing shoulder spines may have deterred predators from attacking and were perhaps also used to attract mates.

Ankylosaurs

The ankylosaurs were a group of heavily armored dinosaurs that first appeared in the Jurassic Period. Some species, such as Euoplocephalus (yoo-oh-ploh-KEF-a-luss), had enormous tail clubs, which they swung as defensive weapons.

Euoplocephalus

This is the only known fossil of Borealopelta, but it shows the amazing details of its armor.

Pachycephalosaurus

(pak-ee-sef-a-lo-SOR-uss)

Meaning "thick-headed lizard," Pachycephalosaurus is the largest known member of the pachycephalosaurs, which all had incredibly thick, bony skulls. It had teeth for chewing plants, but evidence suggests it may also have eaten meat.

» **Length:** 16 ft (5 m)
» **Diet:** Herbivore or omnivore
» **Period:** Cretaceous
» **Location:** North America

A thick, domed head made from solid bone was surrounded with spikes. It was most likely used to ram opponents.

Pachycephalosaurus's wide body may have protected its internal organs if it was butted in the side.

A long, rigid tail helped to keep Pachycephalosaurus balanced as it walked on two legs.

A tough beak was used to grab plants, seeds, and fruit.

No complete skeletons have been found of this dinosaur.

Bighorn sheep

Headbutting

Many living animals, such as bighorn sheep, compete by headbutting each other to prove their strength and attract a mate. Pachycephalosaurs likely took part in headbutting contests, and the spongy bone inside their skulls would have absorbed the shocks when they clashed together.

The domed skull was incredibly strong and could be up to an amazing 10 in (25 cm) thick.

Triceratops

(try-SEH-ra-tops)

The first Triceratops was discovered in 1887 and was mistaken for a type of giant prehistoric bison. Triceratops was among the very last of the horned dinosaurs and became extinct at the end of the Cretaceous Period.

» **Length:** 30 ft (9 m)
» **Diet:** Herbivore
» **Period:** Cretaceous
» **Location:** North America

The large frill might have been colorful and used in displays.

Triceratops means "three-horned face." It had two brow horns and a nose horn.

Triceratops used its parrotlike beak to collect tough vegetation, which was chewed up with hundreds of teeth.

The large body weighed four times as much as a fully grown rhinoceros.

At about 8 ft (2.5 m) long, Triceratops' skull is among the largest of any land animal ever.

Pentaceratops

Pentaceratops (pen-ta-SEH-ra-tops) had an enormous bony frill, much longer than that of Triceratops. It also had five horns rather than three, including two small horns on its cheeks. Its name means "five-horned face."

Pentaceratops

Psittacosaurus

(si-ta-kuh-SOR-uss)

Psittacosaurus and Triceratops belonged to the same group of dinosaurs, called ceratopsians. One extraordinary fossil of Psittacosaurus found in China had parts of its skin preserved, which allowed scientists to determine what color it was.

» **Length:** 6½ ft (2 m)
» **Diet:** Herbivore
» **Period:** Cretaceous
» **Location:** Asia

Unlike other ceratopsians, Psittacosaurus didn't have brow horns. It had two cheek horns, one on each side of its face.

A brush of quill-like bristles ran along its lower back and tail and may have been used for display.

Psittacosaurus had a birdlike beak. Its name means "parrot lizard."

Younger Psittacosaurus may have used all four legs to walk, whereas adults walked on their back legs.

This Psittacosaurus skull shows the teeth hidden behind the dinosaur's beak.

Hiding in plain sight

The skin of Psittacosaurus shows that it was dark on top and light underneath. This type of coloration is known as countershading. It helps animals, such as Thomson's gazelle, blend into their surroundings when lit from above by the sun.

Thomson's gazelle

Tyrannosaurus

(tai-ran-oh-SOR-uss)

Meaning "tyrant lizard," Tyrannosaurus is probably the most famous of all the dinosaurs. This powerful predator was top of the food chain and weighed more than an adult African elephant. More than 50 skeletons have been found, including almost complete individuals.

» **Length:** 43 ft (13 m)
» **Diet:** Carnivore
» **Period:** Cretaceous
» **Location:** North America

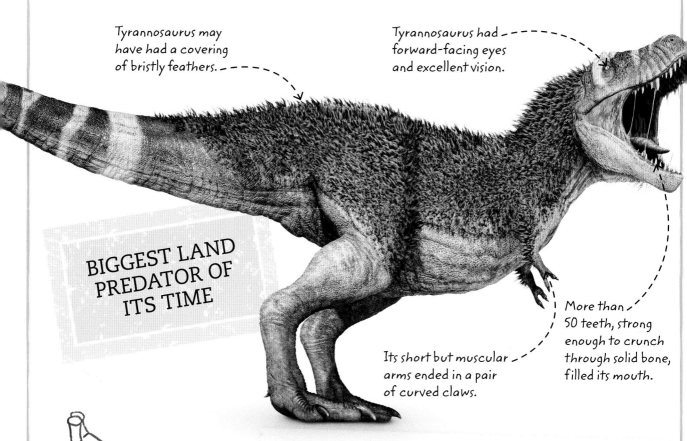

Tyrannosaurus may have had a covering of bristly feathers.

Tyrannosaurus had forward-facing eyes and excellent vision.

BIGGEST LAND PREDATOR OF ITS TIME

More than 50 teeth, strong enough to crunch through solid bone, filled its mouth.

Its short but muscular arms ended in a pair of curved claws.

Some of Tyrannosaurus's teeth were about as long as bananas.

Scary skull

Tyrannosaurus's deep jaws had strong muscles attached to them. These muscles gave it an extremely powerful bite—about 10 times more powerful than that of an alligator.

Tyrannosaurus skull

Spinosaurus

(spy-noh-SOR-uss)

Spinosaurus is the largest carnivorous dinosaur ever discovered—and also one of the most unusual. It had a tall sail on its back and a finlike tail. It lived both on land and in the water, where it spent time swimming in rivers and lakes.

Fact file

» **Length:** 50 ft (16 m)
» **Diet:** Carnivore
» **Period:** Cretaceous
» **Location:** Africa

A crocodile-like snout filled with sharp, conical teeth suggests that Spinosaurus ate fish.

The sail was supported by tall bony spines. It may have helped Spinosaurus warm up and cool down, make it look more intimidating, or attract a mate.

Three long curved claws on each hand may have been used to hook fish out of the water, and to fight.

Spinosaurus dined on huge fish such as the car-sized Mawsonia (maw-SOH-nee-a).

Sailfin lizard

Studying modern animals can help us learn about prehistoric animals. The male Philippine sailfin lizard has a sail on its back a bit like Spinosaurus. It also has a finlike tail, which helps it to swim.

Philippine sailfin lizard

71

The asteroid

Around 66 million years ago, an enormous asteroid, thought to have been up to 10 miles (16 km) wide, struck the Earth. It hit the planet with such force that it wiped out most life and brought the reign of the dinosaurs to a dramatic and abrupt end.

Three-quarters of all animals on Earth died because of the asteroid.

The direct impact resulted in massive tidal waves, an unbearable heat wave, and chunks of hot debris being flung into the air.

Dinosaurs and any other animals and plants close to the impact zone were obliterated within seconds. Hot rocks and dust clouded the skies and started forest fires.

The asteroid left behind a crater about 100 miles (160 km) wide, known as the Chicxulub crater. Today, it lies hidden beneath the Yucatán Peninsula in Mexico.

End of an era

The deadly impact triggered one of the worst mass extinction events of all time. A huge range of organisms, big and small, were killed. All large land animals disappeared and the only survivors were those that could find shelter and adapt.

The pterosaurs, which had long mastered the skies, became extinct as a direct result of the asteroid hit.

The last big dinosaurs, such as Triceratops, died out. However, one group of dinosaurs survived—the tiny birds that quickly adapted to the new world.

Plesiosaurs and mosasaurs, the marine reptiles that had dominated the oceans for millions of years, were eliminated.

Archaeopteryx

(ar-kee-OP-ter-iks)

The first skeleton of Archaeopteryx was found in Germany in 1861. With a mix of reptile and bird features, it was the first fossil to hint at a link between dinosaurs and birds—making it one of the most important dinosaur discoveries ever.

Fact file

» **Length:** 20 in (50 cm)
» **Diet:** Carnivore
» **Period:** Jurassic
» **Location:** Europe

Archaeopteryx had claws on its wings that it may have used to climb through trees.

Unlike modern birds, this birdlike dinosaur had numerous small, sharp teeth in its jaws.

Archaeopteryx could fly, but not very well. It would have glided from tree to tree in search of food.

Studies of color pigments trapped inside Archaeopteryx feathers have shown that they were at least partly black.

Sinosauropteryx

Feather colors

Scientists can now determine what color some dinosaurs were from fossilized skin and feathers that contain color pigments. Sinosauropteryx (sai-noh-sor-OP-teh-riks) had an orange-and-white striped tail and was darker on top and lighter underneath.

More than 10 Archaeopteryx fossils have been discovered and several preserve amazing details of their wings.

Phorusrhacos

(fo-russ-RA-koss)

One of the top predators of its day, Phorusrhacos was a member of a group of giant flightless birds called "terror birds." It preyed upon various animals including dog-sized horses, which it most likely ambushed.

» **Height:** 8 ft (2.5 m)
» **Diet:** Carnivore
» **Period:** Neogene
» **Location:** South America

Its wings were very small, but they had hooklike claws that may have been used during close combat.

Phorusrhacos may have hit top speeds of 30 mph (50 kph).

A sharp beak was used to stab and peck at prey before tearing it into pieces.

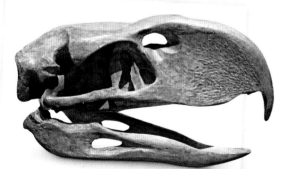

Fearsome fossil

Phorusrhacos had a giant skull that was 24 in (60 cm) or more in length. Similar to birds of prey, it had an upper beak with a sharply hooked point for tearing up meat.

Long powerful legs made Phorusrhacos a speedy hunter.

Its large, sharp claws made for deadly weapons as it kicked at prey and other Phorusrhacos.

Megazostrodon

(meh-ga-ZOSS-tro-don)

While dinosaurs ruled the land, early mammals lived in their shadows. Scurrying on the floor and climbing up trees, the shrew-sized Megazostrodon was probably one of the first mammals, or at least a close relative of the mammals.

» **Length:** 4 in (10 cm)
» **Diet:** Carnivore
» **Period:** Jurassic
» **Location:** Africa and Europe

Megazostrodon may have been nocturnal, meaning it was awake at night.

A fluffy covering of fur stopped body heat from escaping and kept Megazostrodon warm.

Sharp teeth were used to snap up squishy worms, crunchy insects, and even small lizards.

Scientists aren't sure if Megazostrodon had a furry tail, or a scaly one like modern rats.

Echidna egg

Egg-laying mammals

Megazostrodon probably laid leathery-shelled eggs. This unusual feature is seen in a group of modern mammals called monotremes, which include the platypus and echidnas. Megazostrodon babies probably fed on milk from their mothers.

Platybelodon

(pla-ti-BEL-o-don)

Platybelodon belonged to a family of bizarre elephant relatives commonly known as "shovel-tuskers." They had shovel-like tusks in their lower jaws, but rather than being used for digging, the tusks were used to strip bark from trees and slice up tough plants.

» **Length:** 10 ft (3 m)
» **Diet:** Herbivore
» **Period:** Neogene
» **Location:** Africa, Asia, Europe, and North America

The largest Platybelodon were slightly smaller than an African elephant.

Just like an elephant, Platybelodon used its trunk for many things, including feeding and drinking.

Fossils show that males had much longer upper tusks than females.

The unusual flat lower tusks stuck out from Platybelodon's long lower jaw.

Deinotherium

Another ancient relative of elephants, Deinotherium (dai-no-THEER-ee-um) did not have any upper tusks but did have a pair of backward-curved lower tusks. These were probably used to pull branches down so they could feed on the leaves.

Deinotherium

This female Platybelodon skull shows its shorter upper tusks.

77

Ice ages

An ice age is a period of time where the Earth's temperature drops so dramatically that huge amounts of water become frozen on land as ice. The Earth has experienced many ice ages, each of which lasted for millions of years at a time.

700 million years ago, the planet was covered entirely in ice—a "snowball Earth."

Arctodus (ark-TOH-duss)

At the peak of the last ice age, vast ice sheets blanketed much of the northern hemisphere.

The Ice Age

The last ice age, known simply as the "Ice Age," reached its peak roughly 21,000 years ago. Temperatures during an ice age are not always below zero and we are, in fact, still in the Ice Age. At this stage, though, the world has warmed enough that only the poles are covered in ice.

Ice Age animals

To survive during the Ice Age, animals needed to adapt to the low temperatures. However, when the ocean froze and sea levels dropped, new routes between land masses were revealed that allowed species to venture far and wide to new places.

Mammoths and mastodons looked similar, but mastodons had noticeably straighter tusks.

Mastodon
(MASS-tuh-don)

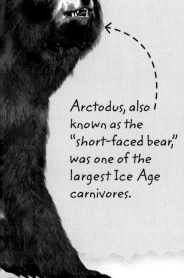

Arctodus, also known as the "short-faced bear," was one of the largest Ice Age carnivores.

Coelodonta (see-lo-DON-ta)

Coelodonta, or the woolly rhinoceros, had a furry coat to keep it warm.

The Ukok Plateau in Russia has a similar environment to the mammoth steppe.

Mammoth steppe

Large open grasslands, known as mammoth steppe, were a key habitat of the Ice Age. Here, vast herds of herbivores, including mammoths and bison, were hunted by top predators, such as saber-toothed cats and early humans.

Megaloceros

(meh-ga-LOSS-eh-ross)

The mighty Megaloceros, a giant deer, was a target for human hunters and it became extinct around 8,000 years ago. It is known from thousands of fossils. Adult males had enormous antlers that could be as wide as their body was long.

» **Length:** 11 ft (3.5 m)
» **Diet:** Herbivore
» **Period:** Quaternary
» **Location:** Asia and Europe

LARGEST DEER EVER TO LIVE

Megaloceros probably used its antlers as weapons during fights between males for mates.

Strong legs made Megaloceros a fast runner, capable of covering long distances.

Megaloceros's huge antlers were made of bone. They fell off and regrew each year.

Moose

Moose

The moose is the largest and heaviest deer living today, with antlers measuring up to 6½ ft (2 m) across. Male moose also regrow their antlers every year.

Mammuthus

(MA-muh-thuss)

Not all Mammuthus, also called mammoths, had a hairy coat or lived in freezing conditions, but the woolly mammoth did. The last remaining woolly mammoths were still alive when the Great Pyramid of Giza was built by the ancient Egyptians!

Fact file

» **Length:** 13 ft (4 m)
» **Diet:** Herbivore
» **Period:** Quaternary
» **Location:** Africa, Asia, Europe, and North America

During the Ice Age, people built huts out of mammoth bones.

A thick, shaggy fur coat kept the woolly mammoth warm during the extreme cold of the Ice Age.

Massive tusks were actually extra-long teeth curved inward. They were used for fighting and digging.

Like its living cousins, the elephants, a mammoth had a long trunk that it used to grasp food.

The woolly mammoth had a short tail that was unlikely to get frostbite.

Frozen remains

Lots of mammoths have been found frozen in ice. Many are preserved with their skin, organs, and even their last meal intact. Baby mammoths with milk inside their bellies are known.

A baby mammoth found preserved in ice.

Smilodon

(SMAI-luh-don)

Smilodon is also known as the saber-toothed cat because of its huge canine teeth. They protruded from the upper jaw and were used to stab and slash Smilodon's unlucky prey, which it probably ambushed in surprise attacks.

Powerful muscles in its neck, arms, and legs helped Smilodon to grip and hold struggling prey.

Unlike modern big cats, Smilodon had a short tail.

Sharp pointed tips helped the canine teeth to pierce through flesh.

Thylacosmilus

Although it looked like Smilodon, Thylacosmilus (thai-la-koh-SMAI-luss) was not a cat. It was related to marsupials. Its lower jaw had a bony extension that may have helped to protect its big teeth.

Thylacosmilus

Smilodon had slicing cheek teeth for eating a strict diet of meat.

Glyptodon
(GLIP-tuh-don)

About the size of a small car, but built like a tank, Glyptodon was protected by an immense domed shell covered in more than a thousand bony tiles. Its thick armor was its main form of defense against predators, such as saber-toothed cats.

» **Length:** 11 ft (3.5 m)
» **Diet:** Herbivore
» **Period:** Quaternary
» **Location:** North America and South America

Glyptodon's armor was very heavy. It weighed 2.2 tons (2 metric tons).

Grinding teeth were used to crush up tough vegetation.

A heavily armored tail was covered in rings of bone.

The solid bony tiles, called osteoderms (O-stee-oh-derms), that made up the shell of Glyptodon were about 1 in (2.5 cm) thick.

Armadillo

Glyptodon was a mega-sized prehistoric cousin of modern armadillos. These mammals also have a tough shell and some can even roll into a ball to protect their soft bellies.

Brazilian three-banded armadillo

83

Canis dirus

(KAY-niss DAI-russ)

Canis is the scientific name given to some members of the dog family. Canis dirus, more commonly known as the dire wolf, was a fearsome Ice Age pack hunter and scavenger. It lived at the same time as, and may also have fought, saber-toothed cats.

A keen sense of smell helped the dire wolf track down prey and alert it to any danger from other animals.

Large teeth and massive jaws with powerful muscles were used to grab prey.

Its legs were stockier and slightly shorter than most wolves, which means it was probably not as fast.

The dire wolf was slightly larger and about 25 percent heavier than today's gray wolf.

La Brea Tar Pits

Some 10,000–50,000 years ago, animals became trapped in the sticky tar of the La Brea Tar Pits in California. Amazingly, more than 200,000 dire wolf remains have been discovered at this important fossil site.

Gas creates bubbles in the sticky tar.

Megatherium

(meh-ga-THEER-ee-um)

Fact file

» **Length:** 20 ft (6 m)
» **Diet:** Herbivore
» **Period:** Neogene
» **Location:** South America

The elephant-sized Megatherium was one of the largest sloths that ever lived and the biggest-ever land mammal found in South America. Unlike modern species, this giant was a ground sloth that excavated and lived in enormous burrows.

We know that some ground sloths had dark or light brown fur because remains have been discovered deep inside caves.

Huge claws were used to dig underground burrows. Lots of fossilized burrows with claw marks matching those of a ground sloth have been found.

A short, heavy tail helped support its massive body when standing upright to feed on leaves and fruit from treetops.

Sloths

Modern sloths live in trees and are found in the tropical rain forests of Central and South America. Compared with their ancient cousins, living sloths are tiny and rarely exceed 11 lb (5 kg) in weight.

Three-toed sloth

Some of the first Megatherium fossils were discovered in Argentina by English scientist Charles Darwin in 1832.

85

Early humans

Today, our species—Homo sapiens—is the only surviving member of a group of primates that appeared in Africa between 2 and 3 million years ago. Studying fossils of different human species helps us to understand how we evolved.

Humans through time

A human is any member of the 10 or more species belonging to the group Homo, which evolved from an apelike ancestor. Some human species even existed at the same time.

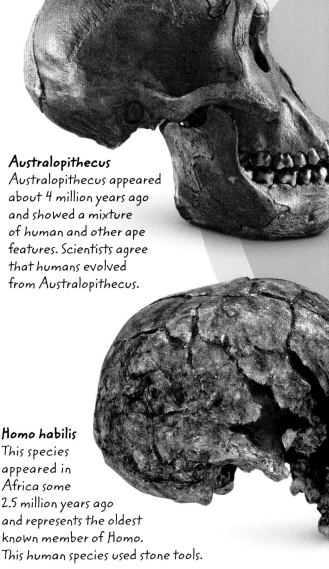

Australopithecus
Australopithecus appeared about 4 million years ago and showed a mixture of human and other ape features. Scientists agree that humans evolved from Australopithecus.

Learning to walk

A major turning point in the evolution of early humans was the ability to walk upright on two legs. This meant they no longer had to live in trees and were able to develop the ability to run, which became vital when hunting.

Australopithecus was one of the first apes to walk upright.

Homo habilis
This species appeared in Africa some 2.5 million years ago and represents the oldest known member of Homo. This human species used stone tools.

Homo sapiens

Modern humans evolved in Africa between 200,000 and 300,000 years ago. A big brain allowed modern humans to solve complex problems and work together in social groups.

Using tools

Bigger brains meant early humans learned to make and use tools. The earliest evidence of stone scrapers and hammers is 2.5 million years old. Tools helped early humans hunt, catch, and cut up their prey.

Hand ax replica

Homo neanderthalensis

Homo neanderthalensis, also known as the Neanderthal, went extinct around 40,000 years ago. Evidence shows that some Neanderthals had children with Homo sapiens.

Homo erectus

Homo erectus appeared around 2 million years ago. Fossils show this human species lived in Africa, Asia, and Europe, and was as tall as Homo sapiens.

Cave paintings by early humans show extinct animals, such as mammoths.

Extinction

When a species dies out, it is considered to be extinct and is gone forever. Extinctions may happen for several reasons, including a global catastrophic event—such as the dinosaur-destroying asteroid—climate change, hunting, rising sea levels, and habitat loss.

Fossil evidence suggests that woolly mammoths were hunted to extinction by early humans. They ate the mammoth meat, and built tools and homes from the bones.

The mammoth's main form of defense against attack was its gigantic curved tusks that could deliver a deadly blow.

Working together, early humans successfully hunted even the largest land mammals, like the woolly mammoth.

Recent extinctions

Humans are among the deadliest predators on the planet and have caused the extinction of many animals. Today, species including the black rhinoceros and Bornean orangutan are at risk of becoming extinct unless they are given help.

The thylacine, or "Tasmanian tiger," was a wolflike marsupial. After excessive hunting and habitat destruction, the last one died in 1936.

Moa were large flightless birds from New Zealand. When humans arrived, they hunted moa, which became extinct more than 500 years ago.

The dodo had no predators until sailors and their animals arrived on the island of Mauritius. This bird became extinct in the late 1600s.

All together

This book shows off just some of the thousands of prehistoric plants and animals that have been discovered. Here, you'll find a selection of the organisms shown in the book and how to say their names.

Araucaria
(a-row-KAIR-ee-a)
pg. 18

Williamsonia
(wil-yem-SOH-nee-a)
pg. 19

Asteroxylon
(AS-ter-ox-y-lon)
pg. 20

Pleuromeia
(ploo-roh-MAY-a)
pg. 20

Sigillaria
(si-ji-LAIR-ee-a)
pg. 21

Lepidodendron
(leh-pi-doh-DEN-dron)
pg. 21

Tempskya
(temp-SKI-a)
pg. 22

Magnolia
(mag-NOH-lee-a)
pg. 23

Dickinsonia
(dik-in-SOH-nee-a)
pg. 26

Hallucigenia
(ha-loo-si-JEE-nee-a)
pg. 27

Paraceraurus
(pa-ra-seh-ROR-uss)
pg. 28

Anomalocaris
(a-nom-a-loh-KAR-iss)
pg. 29

Heliophyllum
(hee-lee-oh-FAI-lum)
pg. 30

Encrinus
(en-KRY-nuss)
pg. 31

Eurypterus
(yoo-RIP-teh-russ)
pg. 32

Mesolimulus
(mez-oh-LIM-yoo-luss)
pg. 33

Scaphites
(skaf-AI-teez)
pg. 34

Cylindroteuthis
(si-LIN-dro-too-thiss)
pg. 35

Arthropleura
(arth-ro-PLOO-ra)
pg. 36

Meganeura
(meh-ga-NYOO-ra)
pg. 37

Dunkleosteus
(dun-KEL-oss-tee-uss)
pg. 38

Cephalaspis
(ke-fa-LASP-iss)
pg. 39

Helicoprion
(hel-i-ko-PRY-on)
pg. 40

Megalodon
(MEH-ga-lo-don)
pg. 41

Tiktaalik
(tik-TAH-lik)
pg. 44

Metoposaurus
(meh-to-po-SOR-uss)
pg. 45

Dimetrodon
(dai-MET-roh-don)
pg. 46

Varanus priscus
(VA-ra-nuss PRIS-kuss)
pg. 47

Shonisaurus
(sho-nee-SOR-uss)
pg. 48

Mixosaurus
(mik-so-SOR-uss)
pg. 48

Ophthalmosaurus
(op-thal-mo-SOR-uss)
pg. 49

Stenopterygius
(steh-nop-tuh-RI-jee-uss)
pg. 49

Ichthyosaurus
(ik-thee-uh-SOR-uss)
pg. 49

Mosasaurus
(moh-za-SOR-uss)
pg. 50

Zarafasaura
(za-ra-fuh-SOR-a)
pg. 51

Deinosuchus
(dai-no-SOO-kuss)
pg. 52

Titanoboa
(tai-tan-oh-BOH-a)
pg. 53

Quetzalcoatlus
(kwets-ul-koh-AT-luss)
pg. 54

Pterodaustro
(teh-ruh-DOR-stroh)
pg. 55

Tupandactylus
(too-pan-DAK-ti-luss)
pg. 55

Pterodactylus
(teh-ruh-DAK-ti-luss)
pg. 55

Rhamphorhynchus
(ram-fo-RINK-uss)
pg. 55

Eodromaeus
(ee-oh-dro-MAY-uss)
pg. 58

Stegosaurus
(steh-guh-SOR-uss)
pg. 59

Velociraptor
(veh-loss-i-RAP-tuh)
pg. 60

Deinocheirus
(dai-no-KAI-russ)
pg. 61

Iguanodon
(ig-WAH-nuh-don)
pg. 62

Parasaurolophus
(pa-ra-sor-uh-LOH-fuss)
pg. 63

Amargasaurus
(a-mar-ga-SOR-uss)
pg. 64

Diplodocus
(dip-LOD-o-kuss)
pg. 64

Mamenchisaurus
(ma-men-chee-SOR-uss)
pg. 65

Argentinosaurus
(ar-jen-tee-no-SOR-uss)
pg. 65

Giraffatitan
(ji-raf-a-TAI-tan)
pg. 65

Borealopelta
(bor-ee-al-oh-PEL-ta)
pg. 66

Pachycephalo-saurus
(pak-ee-sef-a-lo-SOR-uss)
pg. 67

Triceratops
(try-SEH-ra-tops)
pg. 68

Psittacosaurus
(si-ta-kuh-SOR-uss)
pg. 69

Tyrannosaurus
(tai-ran-oh-SOR-uss)
pg. 70

Spinosaurus
(spy-noh-SOR-uss)
pg. 71

Archaeopteryx
(ar-kee-OP-ter-iks)
pg. 74

Phorusrhacos
(fo-russ-RA-koss)
pg. 75

Megazostrodon
(meh-ga-ZOSS-tro-don)
pg. 76

Platybelodon
(pla-ti-BEL-o-don)
pg. 77

Megaloceros
(meh-ga-LOSS-eh-ross)
pg. 80

Mammuthus
(MA-muh-thuss)
pg. 81

Smilodon
(SMAI-luh-don)
pg. 82

Glyptodon
(GLIP-tuh-don)
pg. 83

Canis dirus
(KAY-niss DAI-russ)
pg. 84

Megatherium
(meh-ga-THEER-ee-um)
pg. 85

Glossary

ammonite
type of marine invertebrate with a spiral shell. Related to squid and cuttlefish, ammonites thrived throughout the Mesozoic Era

amphibian
cold-blooded vertebrate that is able to live both on land and in water but lays its eggs in water, such as a frog

ankylosaur
type of plant-eating dinosaur that was heavily armored, such as Borealopelta

ape
type of primate without a tail. The great apes include gorillas and chimpanzees

arthropod
invertebrate with a hard outer skeleton and a segmented body, such as an insect

asteroid
rocky object that orbits the sun. Lots of them are found in our solar system

bird
warm-blooded vertebrate with feathers and a beak that lays hard-shelled eggs, such as an eagle or owl. Birds evolved from theropod dinosaurs

carnivore
animal that gets its food from eating another animal; also called a meat-eater

ceratopsian
type of plant-eating dinosaur that often had enormous horns and a bony frill, such as Triceratops

cone
cone-shaped plant structure containing reproductive spores, pollen, or seeds

dinosaur
member of the successful group of reptiles that appeared in the Triassic Period and held their legs directly beneath their bodies. Dinosaurs exist today as birds

era
named portion of geological time containing lots of different periods

evolution
process whereby one species gives rise to another over many generations

extinction
dying out of a species, which may be caused by different reasons, such as hunting or habitat loss

fish
cold-blooded vertebrate that lives in water and breathes using gills, such as a shark

fossil
remains or traces of a prehistoric organism

herbivore
animal that only eats vegetation; also called a plant-eater

ice age
long stretch of time when global temperatures are relatively cold and large areas of the Earth are covered by ice sheets

ichthyosaur
type of marine reptile, some of which resembled dolphins. Ichthyosaurs appeared at the beginning of the Triassic Period

invertebrate
animal without a backbone

mammal
warm-blooded, hairy vertebrate that produces milk to feed its young, such as a cat or dog

marsupial
type of mammal that looks after its young in a pouch on its stomach, such as a kangaroo

nocturnal
description of an animal that is active at night

ornithopod

type of large or small plant-eating dinosaur, such as Iguanodon. Some ornithopods could walk on either two or four legs

pachycephalosaur

type of dinosaur with a thick skull, such as Pachycephalosaurus. Pachycephalosaurs walked on two legs

paleontologist

scientist who studies the history of life on Earth, usually through the examination of fossils

period

named portion of geological time. Multiple periods make up an era

pigment

natural material that gives an animal or plant its color

pollination

transfer of pollen from one flower to another, so that seeds can be produced. A pollinator is an animal that carries the pollen

predator

animal that preys on other animals for food

preservation

keeping something the same or preventing it from being damaged or destroyed

prey

animal that is hunted and killed by another for food

primitive

at an early stage of evolution or development

pterosaur

type of flying reptile that was the first vertebrate to fly

reptile

cold-blooded, scaly vertebrate, such as a crocodile, snake, or turtle. Reptiles usually lay soft-shelled eggs on land

sauropod

type of plant-eating dinosaur with a long neck and tail, such as Diplodocus

seed

reproductive structure of some plants. Seeds are often tough and new plants sprout from them

spore

tiny reproductive structure of some plants, fungi, and other organisms

stegosaur

plant-eating dinosaur with two rows of armor plates or spines running down the neck, back, and tail, such as Stegosaurus

tectonic plate

giant slab of rock that makes up part of Earth's top layer. Tectonic plates float on a lower liquid layer of molten rock, and move, collide, and slide against each other

tetrapod

four-legged vertebrate, or any animal evolved from it

theropod

type of dinosaur with sharp claws that usually ate meat, such as Tyrannosaurus. Some theropods were herbivores or omnivores

trilobite

type of marine invertebrate with a segmented shell divided into three main parts. Trilobites lived in the Paleozoic Era

tusk

long, greatly enlarged pointed tooth, as seen in animals such as elephants

vertebrate

animal with an internal bony or cartilaginous skeleton, including a skull and backbone

Index

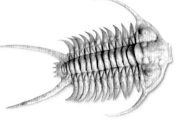

IJK

ice ages 78–79
ichthyosaurs 48–49
Ichthyosaurus 49
Iguanodon 25, 62
invertebrates 25
jet 18
Jurassic Period 8, 11
Komodo dragons 47

L

La Brea Tar Pits 84
Lambeosaurus 63
lampreys 39
Lepidodendron 21
Liopleurodon 51
lizard-hipped dinosaurs 57
lungfish 43
lycophytes 17, 20–21

MN

magnolia 23
Mamenchisaurus 65
mammals 25, 76
mammoths 79, 81, 88–89
Mammuthus 81
mass extinction 72–73
mastodons 79
Megaloceros 80
megalodon 41
Meganeura 37
Megatherium 85
Megazostrodon 76
Mesolimulus 33
Mesozoic Era 8, 56
meteors 4, 5
Metoposaurus 45
microorganisms 5, 6
millipedes 36
Mixosaurus 48
moa 89
moose 80
mosasaurs 50, 73
Mosasaurus 50
mosses 16
nautilus 34
Neogene Period 9

O

Ophthalmosaurus 49
Ordovician Period 9
ornithischians 56
ornithomimosaurs 61
oxygen 4

P

Pachycephalosaurus 67
paleontologists 15, 49
Paleogene Period 8, 11
Paleozoic Era 8–9, 10
Panderichthys 44
Pangaea 10, 11
Paraceraurus 28
Parasaurolophus 63
Pentaceratops 68
periods 8–9
Permian Period 8
Phorusrhacos 75
plants 6–7, 16–17, 43
Platybelodon 77
plesiosaurs 51, 73
Pleuromeia 20
pliosaurs 51
Protoceratops 60
Psittacosaurus 69
Pterodactylus 54–55
pterosaurs 12–13, 54–55, 73

QR

Quaternary Period 9
Quetzalcoatlus 54
reproduction, plants 17
reptiles 25
Rhamphorhynchus 55

S

saber-toothed cat 82
sailfin lizards 71
saurischians 57
Sauropelta 56
sauropods 57, 64–65
Scaphites 34
sea scorpions 32
Shonisaurus 48

Sigillaria 20–21
Silurian Period 9
Sinosauropteryx 74
sloths 85
Smilodon 82
snakes 53
Spinosaurus 71
squid 35
stegosaurs 56, 59
Stegosaurus 56, 59
Stenopterygius 49
stromatolites 5
Struthiomimus 61
supercontinents 10

T

tectonic plates 11
teeth 25
Tempskya 22
tetrapods 42, 43
theropods 57
thylacine 89
Thylacosmilus 82
Tiktaalik 42, 43, 44
Titanoboa 53
tools 87
trace fossils 13
Triassic Period 8
Triceratops 68, 73
Tupandactylus 55
Tyrannosaurus 70

VWZ

Varanus priscus 47
Velociraptor 25, 60
velvet worms 27
Wallace, Alfred Russel 7
Williamsonia 19
woolly mammoths 81,
  88–89
Zarafasaura 51

Acknowledgments

Dean Lomax would like to thank Natalie Turner for reviewing the first version of this book.

Dorling Kindersley would like to thank Marie Greenwood for editorial assistance, Bettina Myklebust Stovne for illustration, Peter Minister and James Kuether for CGI illustration, Simon Mumford for cartography, Caroline Hunt for proofreading, and Helen Peters for the index.

The publisher would like to thank the following for their kind permission to reproduce their photographs:

(Key: a-above; b-below/bottom; c-center; f-far; l-left; r-right; t-top)

2 Dorling Kindersley: Jon Hughes (bc). **Dreamstime.com:** Alexander Potapov (tc). **4–5 Dreamstime.com:** Supakit Kumwiwat (background). **Science Photo Library:** Lynette Cook. **5 Alamy Stock Photo:** Jane Gould (crb); Science History Images / Photo Researchers (cra). **6 123RF.com:** Corey A Ford (br). **Alamy Stock Photo:** Science Photo Library / Steve Gschmeissner (c). **Dreamstime.com:** Alexander Potapov (bl). **6–7 Dreamstime.com:** Supakit Kumwiwat. **7 123RF.com:** Corey A Ford (tr). **Alamy Stock Photo:** Nigel Cattlin (cb). **Dorling Kindersley:** James Kuether (ca). **Science Photo Library:** Claus Lunau (br). **8 Dreamstime.com:** Mopic (tr). **8–9 Dreamstime.com:** Supakit Kumwiwat. **9 Alamy Stock Photo:** John Cancalosi (br); Universal Images Group North America LLC / DeAgostini (tr). **Dorling Kindersley:** James Kuether (cr). **Dreamstime.com:** Corey A Ford (tl). **10–11 Dreamstime.com:** Supakit Kumwiwat. **11 Alamy Stock Photo:** Derek Trask (tl). **12–13 Dreamstime.com:** Supakit Kumwiwat (background). **Science Photo Library:** Dirk Wiersma. **13 Dorling Kindersley:** Natural History Museum, London (cra). **14–15 Dreamstime.com:** Supakit Kumwiwat. **15 Alamy Stock Photo:** incamerastock / ICP (cra). **Dorling Kindersley:** Oxford University Museum of Natural History (tl). **16 Dreamstime.com:** Johannesk (bc); suriya silsaksom khunaspix@yahoo.co.th (tr). **16–17 Dreamstime.com:** Supakit Kumwiwat. **17 123RF.com:** Koosen (cra). **Alamy Stock Photo:** Don Johnston_WU (br). **Dreamstime.com:** Jolanta Dabrowska (tl); Irochka (c). **Getty Images:** Paul Starosta (tc). **18 Alamy Stock Photo:** Dominic Jones (r). **19 Alamy Stock Photo:** Hoberman Publishing (crb). **Dorling Kindersley:** Natural History Museum, London (bl). **20–21 Dreamstime.com:** Supakit Kumwiwat. **21 Dorling Kindersley:** Oxford Museum of Natural History (cr); Swedish Museum of Natural History (bc). **22 Dreamstime.com:** Corey A Ford (bl). **23 Alamy Stock Photo:** Zoonar GmbH (bl). **Dreamstime.com:** Alexander Potapov (cra). **24 123RF.com:** Corey A Ford (bl). **24–25 Dreamstime.com:** Supakit Kumwiwat. **25 123RF.com:** Sebastian Kaulitzki (bc). **Dorling Kindersley:** Natural History Museum, London (ca). **iStockphoto.com:** Mark Kostich (cra). **Science Photo Library:** Jaime Chirinos (c). **26 Alamy Stock Photo:** Universal Images Group North America LLC / DeAgostini (clb); Dotted Zebra (cr). **27 Alamy Stock Photo:** Eng Wah Teo (bc). **Dreamstime.com:** Planetfelicity (c). **28 Alamy Stock Photo:** Jason Bazzano (br); Ivan Vdovin (bl). **Science Photo Library:** Walter Myers (c). **29 Dorling Kindersley:** James Kuether (c). **30 iStockphoto.com:** vlad61 (br). **31 Alamy Stock Photo:** Wild Places Photography / Chris Howes (cra). **Dr Dean Lomax:** Bielefeld Natural History Museum (clb). **Science Photo Library:** Georgette Douwma (br). **32 Alamy Stock Photo:** Stocktrek Images, Inc. / Nobumichi Tamura (cb). **Dreamstime.com:** Corey A Ford (bl). **33 Dr Dean Lomax:** Wyoming Dinosaur Center (crb). **Dreamstime.com:** Andriy Bezuglov (bc). **34 Dorling Kindersley:** Oxford University Museum of Natural History (cl). **Dreamstime.com:** Eugene Sim Junying (br). **35 Shutterstock.com:** Dan Bagur (br). **36 Dreamstime.com:** Corey A Ford (cr). **37 123RF.com:** Corey A Ford. **Fotolia:** Roque141 (cr). **38 Alamy Stock Photo:** All Canada Photos / Stephen J. Krasemann (bl). **39 Alamy Stock Photo:** Sabena Jane Blackbird (bl); Stocktrek Images, Inc. / Nobumichi Tamura (c); Nature Photographers Ltd / Paul R. Sterry (br). **40 Dorling Kindersley:** Natural History Museum, London (bl). **Dreamstime.com:** Wrangel (br). **Science Photo Library:** Mikkel Juul Jensen (c). **41 Dorling Kindersley:** Natural History Museum, London (bc). **Dreamstime.com:** Mark Turner (c); Willtu (bl). **42 Alamy Stock Photo:** Science History Images / Gwen Shockey (cra). **42–43 Dorling Kindersley:** James Kuether (c). **Dreamstime.com:** Supakit Kumwiwat. **43 Alamy Stock Photo:** Paulo Oliveira (cr). **Science Photo Library:** Richard Bizley (tr). **44 Dorling Kindersley:** James Kuether (cb). **45 Science Photo Library:** Millard H. Sharp (br). **46 Alamy Stock Photo:** Corbin17 (cl). **Dorling Kindersley:** James Kuether (br). **47 Dorling Kindersley:** Natural History Museum, London (bl). **Dreamstime.com:** Anna Kucherova / Photomaru (br). **48 James Kuether:** (cb). **48–49 Alamy Stock Photo:** Science Photo Library / Mark Garlick (t). **Dreamstime.com:** Supakit Kumwiwat. **James Kuether:** (c). **50 Alamy Stock Photo:** Phil Degginger (bl); Mohamad Haghani (c). **Science Photo Library:** Sinclair Stammers (br). **51 123RF.com:** Mark Turner (cr). **Dorling Kindersley:** Jon Hughes (br). **Dr Dean Lomax:** Wyoming Dinosaur Center (cl). **52 Alamy Stock Photo:** National Geographic Image Collection (br). **Dreamstime.com:** Mikhail Blajenov / Starper (clb). **53 Alamy Stock Photo:** Michael Wheatley / sculpture by Charlie Brinson (crb). **Dreamstime.com:** Mark Turner (c). **54 Dreamstime.com:** Corey A Ford (tr). **54–55 Dreamstime.com:** Supakit Kumwiwat. **55 Dorling Kindersley:** Jon Hughes (br); Natural History Museum, London (cr). **56–57 Dreamstime.com:** Supakit Kumwiwat. **58 Dreamstime.com:** Leonello Calvetti (crb). **59 Dorling Kindersley:** Natural History Museum, London (crb). **60 Science Photo Library:** Dirk Wiersma (br). **61 Alamy Stock Photo:** The Natural History Museum, London (bl). **Dreamstime.com:** Linda Bucklin (cb). **62 Dorling Kindersley:** Natural History Museum (clb). **63 Dorling Kindersley:** Natural History Museum, London (bl). **64 123RF.com:** Corey A Ford (cr). **Dorling Kindersley:** Senckenberg Gesellschaft Fuer Naturforschung Museum (clb). **64–65 Dreamstime.com:** Supakit Kumwiwat. **66 James Kuether:** (c). **Image Courtesy of the Royal Tyrrell Museum, Drumheller, AB:** (crb). **67 Alamy Stock Photo:** Minden Pictures / Donald M. Jones (crb). **Dorling Kindersley:** Oxford Museum of Natural History (bl). **68 Dorling Kindersley:** Natural History Museum, London (clb). **69 Dorling Kindersley:** Greg and Yvonne Dean (br); James Kuether (c). **70 Alamy Stock Photo:** Leonello Calvetti (c). **Dorling Kindersley:** American Museum of Natural History (br). **71 Dreamstime.com:** Iakov Filimonov (br). **72–73 Alamy Stock Photo:** Science Photo Library / Mark Garlick. **Dreamstime.com:** Supakit Kumwiwat (background). **75 Alamy Stock Photo:** Andrew Rubtsov (clb). **76 Dorling Kindersley:** Booth Museum of Natural History, Brighton (bc). **77 Alamy Stock Photo:** Stocktrek Images, Inc. / Nobumichi Tamura (c). **Science Photo Library:** Science Source / Millard H. Sharp (br). **78 Dorling Kindersley:** NASA / Simon Mumford (bl). **78–79 Dorling Kindersley:** James Kuether (c). **Dreamstime.com:** Supakit Kumwiwat. **79 123RF.com:** Anton Petrus (bl). **Alamy Stock Photo:** Stocktrek Images, Inc. / Nobumichi Tamura (tr). **Dorling Kindersley:** Jon Hughes (c). **80 Alamy Stock Photo:** Accent Alaska.com (crb). **Dorling Kindersley:** Natural History Museum, London (bc). **Science Photo Library:** Roman Uchytel (cb). **81 Alamy Stock Photo:** Aflo Co. Ltd. / Nippon News (bc). **82 Dorling Kindersley:** Natural History Museum, London (br). **Dreamstime.com:** Valentyna Chukhlyebova (c). **83 Alamy Stock Photo:** BIOSPHOTO / Eric Isselee (br). **Dorling Kindersley:** Natural History Museum, London (bl). **84 Alamy Stock Photo:** Martin Shields (br). **Dreamstime.com:** Maria Itina (bl). **85 Dreamstime.com:** Seadam (bc). **86 Alamy Stock Photo:** The Natural History Museum, London (br). **Dorling Kindersley:** Oxford Museum of Natural History (c). **Science Photo Library:** Mauricio Anton (clb). **86–87 Dreamstime.com:** Supakit Kumwiwat. **87 Dorling Kindersley:** Natural History Museum, London (bl); Royal Pavilion & Museums, Brighton & Hove (cr). **Science Photo Library:** Paul Rapson (cla). **88–89 Dreamstime.com:** Supakit Kumwiwat. **89 Depositphotos Inc:** PhotosVac (cra). **Dreamstime.com:** Corey A Ford (br). **90 123RF.com:** Corey A Ford (cb/Meganeura). **Alamy Stock Photo:** Dominic Jones (cla); Dotted Zebra (cl); Stocktrek Images, Inc. / Nobumichi Tamura (cr, crb). **Dorling Kindersley:** James Kuether (c, bl/Tiktaalik). **Dreamstime.com:** Corey A Ford (cra, cb); Planetfelicity (cl/Hallucigenia); Mark Turner (bl). **James Kuether:** (br, br/Mixosaurus). **Science Photo Library:** Mikkel Juul Jensen (crb/Helicoprion); Walter Myers (cl/Paraceraurus). **90–91 Dreamstime.com:** Supakit Kumwiwat. **91 123RF.com:** Corey A Ford (c); Mark Turner (tc). **Alamy Stock Photo:** Leonello Calvetti (cb/T-rex); Science Photo Library / Mark Garlick (tl); Stocktrek Images, Inc. / Nobumichi Tamura (bl); Mohamad Haghani (tc/Mosasaurus). **Dorling Kindersley:** Jon Hughes (ca); James Kuether (cb). **Dreamstime.com:** Linda Bucklin (cra); Mark Turner (tr); Corey A Ford (cla); Valentyna Chukhlyebova (bc/Sabertooth). **James Kuether:** (clb). **Science Photo Library:** Roman Uchytel (bc). **92 123RF.com:** Corey A Ford (tr). **James Kuether:** (bl). **92–93 Dreamstime.com:** Supakit Kumwiwat. **94 Alamy Stock Photo:** Ivan Vdovin (tc). **Dorling Kindersley:** Oxford University Museum of Natural History (bl). **94–95 Dreamstime.com:** Supakit Kumwiwat. **96 Brian Fernando:** (br). **Dreamstime.com:** Supakit Kumwiwat.

Cover images: *Front:* **Alamy Stock Photo:** Leonello Calvetti crb; **Dorling Kindersley:** Oxford University Museum of Natural History tc; **Dreamstime.com:** Valentyna Chukhlyebova tl, Corey A Ford cb; *Back:* **Alamy Stock Photo:** dotted zebra cra/ (Dickinsonia), ca, Andrew Rubtsov tc; **Dorling Kindersley:** Jon Hughes cra, Oxford University Museum of Natural History c; **Dreamstime.com:** Alexander Potapov bc; **Science Photo Library:** Dirk Wiersma tr, cb; *Spine:* **Dorling Kindersley:** Oxford University Museum of Natural History t/ (Ammonite); **Science Photo Library:** Dirk Wiersma t.

Endpaper images: *Front:* **123RF.com:** Mark Turner cb; **Alamy Stock Photo:** Leonello Calvetti fcl, Nigel Cattlin ca, dotted zebra c, Mohamad Haghani fcr, Stocktrek Images, Inc. / Nobumichi Tamura tc, Universal Images Group North America LLC / DeAgostini tl; **Dorling Kindersley:** Jon Hughes ftr; **Dreamstime.com:** Corey A Ford ftl, Alexander Potapov bl, Mark Turner fclb; **Science Photo Library:** Jaime Chirinos ca (Teratorn); *Back:* **Alamy Stock Photo:** All Canada Photos / Stephen J. Krasemann tr (Dunkleosteus), Corbin17 br, Phil Degginger ftl, Andrew Rubtsov fcla (Skull); **Dorling Kindersley:** American Museum of Natural History cb (T-rex), Natural History Museum clb, Natural History Museum, London tr, cr, fcla, bl, tc (Triceratops), tc (Megalania), cb, cb (Tooth), bc, Oxford Museum of Natural History fclb, crb, Oxford University Museum of Natural History cra, Swedish Museum of Natural History fcrb; **Getty Images / iStock:** Mark Kostich fcr, c; **Science Photo Library:** Science Source / Millard H. Sharp ftr, Millard H. Sharp ca, Dirk Wiersma tc.

All other images © Dorling Kindersley
For further information see: www.dkimages.com

About the author

Dr. Dean Lomax is a paleontologist and author. He has loved dinosaurs since he was a child and is now a world expert on ichthyosaurs—having named five new species. He often appears as an expert on TV, and has also written *Dinosaurs Discovered* for DK.